André Dias Pires

A Decolonial Perspective on Art Education in Everyday School Life

André Dias Pires

A Decolonial Perspective on Art Education in Everyday School Life

For an epistemic and decolonial disobedience about art in school education

ScienciaScripts

Imprint

Cover image: Provided by the author

This book is a translation from the original published under ISBN 978-613-9-60223-0.

Publisher:
Sciencia Scripts
is a trademark of
Dodo Books Indian Ocean Ltd. and OmniScriptum S.R.L publishing group

120 High Road, East Finchley, London, N2 9ED, United Kingdom
Str. Armeneasca 28/1, office 1, Chisinau MD-2012, Republic of Moldova, Europe
Printed at: see last page
ISBN: 978-620-7-18463-7

SUMMARY

Chapter 1	12
Chapter 2	26
Chapter 3	37
Chapter 4	60

INTRODUCTION: Geographical and Epistemological Discontinuity about Art and Aesthetic Expressions

I'm an elementary school art teacher at a public school on the outskirts of the city.[1]located in Duque de Caxias, Baixada Fluminense. This place, where I have been working professionally since 2006 with the responsibility of educating the boys and girls present there, challenges me every day. Among other things, because I came from a different background, I'm not from there, I don't live there. In this environment that harbors expectations and frustrations, and acting according to my perspectives as a novice teacher, I was there to promote knowledge of art, deepen it and broaden my intimacy with its universe. However, the demands arising from the dialogue with the cultural universe and the aesthetic attunements of the students in those spaces seemed to be different.

In this movement of going to the other and getting to know their universe, I perceive the subalternizing role determined by the difference between what the school offers and the expectations and experiences of the students (SANTOME, 1995; CANDAU, 2008). In the context of art/education, I am referring objectively to the gap that remains virtually unchallenged between the curricular content considered traditional in this area of knowledge and the students' aesthetic knowledge and experiences, as well as local cultural and artistic productions. Based on this observation, I don't intend to deify a supposed "local culture" or "student culture", but I do question the naturalization of the contents in the arts curriculum, to the detriment of other possibilities excluded from this context.

In this sense, I will problematize art that is defined and institutionalized according to the great evolutionary and linear narrative of Euro-American "art history", which remains hegemonic in the way it is promoted in art/education programs, due to the naturalization in which it is received and applied, in such a way as to avoid prospecting and questioning its regimes of truth. Regardless of the more centralized or peripheralized condition of school spaces, this perspective is connected to an autonomist idea of art[2] in its way of relating the political and the aesthetic, which

---

[1] The term 'peripheral school' is not intended to reduce it to a single essentialized characteristic. We understand that such a place is created by political and cultural circumstances. In this sense, both the 'centers' and the 'peripheries' are the result of power struggles and will therefore be configured alternately and concomitantly in the political, symbolic, geographical, spatial, etc. spheres.

[2] The concept of the autonomy of art, developed and consolidated in the 18th century by thinkers such as Kant and Schiller, establishes an order of distinction in the ontological sphere between art and

"advocates that its function is to have no function and to remain independent of any concrete political project" (AGUIRRE, 2011, p.74). In other words, it is "art for art's sake", which almost always keeps it under a naïve and sweetened discourse, treated as a system of truths beyond good and evil. According to this autonomist perspective, aesthetic knowledge is traditionally linked to universalizing narratives, according to aristocratic standards of beauty and sensibility, which, among other things, has made it something separate from the practical world and from knowledge that is considered useful. However,

> The opposition between discredited and protected values and their territoriality in the social diagram quickly reveals the role and importance of the aesthetic element in the articulation of the various arrangements that make the center the center and the rest the rest (VICTORIO FILHO, 2008, p.9).

In this sense, the political in relation to the arts shapes the properties of the spaces of seeing and saying and the characteristics of access to them. According to Aguirre (2011, p. 72), "it is precisely in the distribution of access to material and symbolic space that the aesthetic and the sensible are allied to the political".

However, teaching art from an autonomist and historicist perspective, or from the analysis of formal and stylistic aspects, can be considered relevant in a given context, because it deals with elements that are part of the hegemonic codes and because it represents a way of achieving social recognition and "cultural elevation" in the face of certain conceptions of culture under which the school institution was founded. However, for young students, it is not enough to know that this or that norm represents the existing standard and that it is necessary to learn it. In this sense, Aguirre (2009) points out that young people's contact with the so-called "cultured arts" is limited to the school environment, associating them with "practices derived from duty" (AGUIRRE, 2009, p.3), an item to be assimilated as a means of gaining a foothold in the adult world. According to the author, the "connection between curricular materials and young people's aesthetic repertoires is completely lacking or non-existent" (AGUIRRE, 2009, p. 3).

For this author, the gap between the school curriculum and the repertoire of the young student would prevent the transformation of high culture products and the visual

---

other objects created by man. This view understands art as a cultural and aesthetically unique element, separating it from functional, pedagogical or moral reasons. In this way, it raises controversy with regard to the regimes of truth on which it relies to determine aesthetic legitimacy (whether something deserves to be treated as art) based on the hegemonic imposition of an ideal driven by an illustrated aristocracy of specialists.

arts into an instrument of relevance to the vital experience of these young people, becoming part of the collection of "school knowledge alien to the world and completely inoperative as shapers of their identity" (AGUIRRE, 2009, p. 3). In this analysis, the author is not strictly referring to young people in peripheral contexts. However, if we frame the discussion in this light, it is even easier to see that such school knowledge about art has little to do with the cultural and symbolic networks that energize the aesthetic attunements of peripheral youth and is therefore largely received with contempt or indifference. In the best of cases, their content is corrupted by the contribution of "the students, who are, despite any belief or law, creators of the curriculum and creators of aesthetic events, if not in the field of art, always in the everyday life of their lives" (VICTORIO FILHO, 2008, p.2-3). However, the hegemonic position of outsourced art remains unchallenged, a source of culturally accepted repertoires that offer apparent security in the form of disciplinary content considered relevant for art classes. In this case, "an impressive universe of cultural, artistic, epistemological, etc. productions remains unqualified, undervalued and discredited" (AGUIRRE, 2008, p.7).

These questions represented a process of changes in my practices, based on trial and error, seeking to interpret and bring art classes closer, from a critical perspective, to the aesthetic expressions that affect the subjectivity of those I have as students. This process was accompanied by the reading of authors concerned with the study of the relationship between art and education and the renewal of this field of knowledge, such as Ana Mae Barbosa, Fernando Hernandez, Imanol Aguirre, Raimundo Martins, Jan Jagodzinski, among others. However, faced with a hectic routine (common to most primary school teachers), with a heavy workload, working with many classes, moving between different schools and locations, I had few opportunities to systematize and deepen this view.

In 2012, after six years of working as an art teacher, I was invited to join the team at the Primary Education Coordination Office (CEF) of the Duque de Caxias Municipal Education Department (SME-Caxias), which was responsible, among other things, for restructuring the curriculum currently in force in the municipal network. Without leaving the classroom, I was given the task of acting as a "moderator" with the other art teachers in the discussions about restructuring the curriculum for this subject. The SME's aim was to revise the municipal network's curriculum proposal, which had been drawn up since 1997 and published in 200433 , as well as other curriculum documents formulated in subsequent revisions. The priority was to define "content matrices" for elementary school subjects, distributed among each year of schooling. This content had to be organized along "thematic axes", forcibly and in detail following the division of content into procedural, conceptual and attitudinal categories, an orientation already indicated in previous drafting processes. My initial process as arts moderator involved reviewing and making proposals based on the existing documents before formally opening the discussion with the other teachers. This situation generated new questions, doubts and challenges in me.

Under the instinctive influence of Multiculturalism, I initially suggested that the thematic axes of the arts curriculum proposal should include two distinct categories: *"Art and its History"* and *"Other Cultures". At* this point, I was trying to ensure that a curriculum document would include a discussion of cultural diversity. In addition, I was following the guidelines contained in the *Duque de Caxias Pedagogical Proposal,* which, among the *General Art Objectives for the 1st and 2nd Segments of Primary Education,* recommends*:* "respecting cultural diversity" and "identifying national and universal artistic movements" (Secretaria Municipal de Educapao-Caxias, 2004 p.61). My aim, then, was to integrate "ethnic content" by adding the study of *"Other Cultures" to the* arts curriculum and to ensure knowledge about the "great works of art", considered "universal heritage".

What I didn't fully realize at the time was that the creation of such thematic axes, as they had been placed, separated into two watertight categories, would reinforce an artificially constructed distinction between "universal culture", represented by the history of Western art, and "the culture of the Other",

> 3 PEDAGOGICAL PROPOSAL. 2ND VOLUME. Secretaria Municipal de Educapao de Duque de Caxias Duque de Caxias, 2004 focused in a fixed way and without dynamism, based on subalternizing signifiers such as handicrafts, folklore, mass and tribal, for example.

The question here is: why do we continue to dichotomously separate the study of culture from those we consider "the Others", "the different", identified by factors relating to social class, gender, ethnicity, sexuality, religion, age, language, in relation to "art history", the official representative of universal culture?

Jagodzinski (2008), problematizing the multicultural art curriculum of *The Getty Center For Education in Arts*[3]addresses a similar issue as follows:

> By placing "Otherness" as a special category of "understanding", showing

[3] The Getty Center for Education in Arts developed "Disciplined-Based-Art Education" (DBAE) which, since the 1960s, has become a reference center for art teacher training in the United States.

> admiration for what is missing in Western culture and art history, the program remains non-threatening as long as this Otherness does not become an active subject, and thus begins to question and define the established course of art history (JAGODZINSKYI, 2008, p. 667).

This accommodation of cultural diversity is described by the author in such a way that the classification of cultures as "the Other" is organized on the basis of the absence of "white". For the author, these calculations are racist even if, at the same time, they appear to be anti-racist. Silva (2014) addresses the issue as follows:

> In a white supremacist society, for example, "being white" is not considered an ethnic or racial identity. In a world governed by US cultural hegemony, "ethnic" is the music or food of other countries. It is homosexual sexuality that is "sexualized", not heterosexual sexuality. **The homogenizing force of normal identity is directly proportional to its invisibility** (SILVA, 2014, p. 83, emphasis added).

In this way, multiculturalism doesn't bring many advantages if it is understood as merely accepting and respecting cultural diversity, from a perspective of "assimilating difference into the traditions and customs of the majority" (HALL, 2006 p.52).

This is a perspective that Hall (2006) calls liberal multiculturalism, which seeks to integrate different cultural groups into the majority society, based on universal individual citizenship, tolerating certain cultural practices of the Other.

As Silva (2014) defines,

> For this perspective, cultural diversity is good and expresses, on the surface, our common human nature. The central problem here is that this approach simply fails to question the power relations and processes of differentiation that, first and foremost, produce identity and difference. In general, the result is the production of new dichotomies, such as the tolerant dominant and the tolerated dominated, or the hegemonic but benevolent identity and the subaltern but "respected" identity (SILVA, 2014, p. 98).

In this way, I realize that curricular proposals apparently surrounded by good intentions such as "respect for cultural diversity" (Secretaria Municipal de Educagao-Caxias, 2004) may, in fact, be helping to perpetuate subalternizing processes, producing new binary logics, reinforcing fetishes and stereotypes in relation to the cultures of the Other of Western modernity. For Jagodzinski (2008),

> Within the very conceptualization of "cultural diversity", there is already a binary of equality/difference at play, which demands more than the declared universal standards of democratic human rights and civil liberties, and which demands anti-racist and anti-oppressive strategies. (JAGODZINSKI, 2008, p.663)

I understand, then, that what appears to many art teachers as an innocent and democratic gesture, which apparently brings "correct" values (appreciation, respect and acceptance of the other's right to be different), while leaving aside a questioning approach to power relations and processes of differentiation, is actually related to a desire for accommodation and consensus in the school context in which difference is interpreted as (benign) diversity and as simple observation. In this case, addressing cultural diversity is, at best, a way of getting to know and reaffirming the pattern and development of hegemonic Western, white and heterosexual culture.

With these questions and seeking to investigate alternatives for other educational narratives in the context of art/education in peripheral school spaces, in 2013 I joined the Postgraduate Program in Education, Culture and Communication in Urban Peripheries at the Baixada Fluminense School of Education of the State University of Rio de Janeiro (FEBF-UERJ). On the university campus, also located in Duque de Caxias, I was introduced to the academic world and to other local worlds that were building my research process. In this way, I matured the questions I was asking, which were reformulated and redesigned with each step I took.

The desire to research arose from the dialog between references, reflections, possibilities and concrete limits of my experiences as an art teacher and, circumstantially, as a proposer of curricular discussions of this subject in elementary school. This situation has given me the opportunity to make contact with part of the group of art teachers in the municipality of Caxias (there are 97 of us in total, distributed among 147 schools in the municipal network). Among other challenges, this has made me think about how my colleagues in other schools face the questions and possibilities I face.

Faced with this possibility of breaking the isolation and establishing a condition of exchange with other art teachers, I see how the problems raised so far about the distance between formal knowledge of art/education (entrenched in the Western and modern canon of art) in relation to the aesthetic and cultural experiences experienced in peripheral school spaces and the questioning of "multicultural" curricular proposals based on universal liberal ethics of inclusion, tolerance and charity - which covertly reinforce and perpetuate processes of cultural domination - are, in fact, intrinsically connected to the colonial civilizing tradition which, in education, promotes an inadvertent naturalization of modern values that predominate in schools and, consequently, in the pedagogical practices of many art teachers. According to this perspective, the "Other" is presented in a subordinate position to the hegemony of the white, Christian and Western man and, in this way, other experiences and knowledge that are considered lesser are excluded from this legitimizing context.

However, the contacts established with other art teachers during my participation as a moderator in curriculum discussions led me to perceive indications that raise alternative possibilities to modern coloniality in art/education. I believe that, despite the intense colonial brand of regulation at work in the school space, other meanings always emerge, presenting non-colonial and contingently emancipatory options. Based on this, I decided to investigate different, critical, culturally emancipatory ways of *doing/knowing* that could be understood as decolonial options for art/education in peripheral school contexts. It's worth saying at the outset that the notion of a "decolonial option"[4] derives from an epistemological, theoretical and political movement for the critical and utopian renewal of social sciences in Latin America which, in the educational field, presents ample possibilities for discussion. Central to the aims of the "decolonial opposition" is the production and legitimization of alternative forms of knowledge to the logic of modernity and the decentring of the colonial epistemic perspective.

Therefore, I am interested in promoting the discussion of possibilities for producing decolonial knowledge-others in the field of art education in peripheral school contexts. To this end, I seek to analyze art teachers' everyday curricular constructions, identifying *doings/knowings* that could represent potential decolonial oppositions in the field of art/education in peripheral school spaces. These *doings/knowings* identified here as potential decolonial oppositions do not, however, constitute conclusive solutions for art/education in the school context, but rather represent indications, characterized by being diffuse, fleeting, fluent and banal, and which, for this very reason, go unnoticed. Based on this understanding, in this research, knowledge aims to be built from the observation of these *doings/knowings,* which present clues, as Ginzburg (1989, apud AMARO, 2014) informs us, "perhaps infinitesimal clues that make it possible to grasp a deeper reality, otherwise unattainable". I believe, therefore, that by investigating emancipatory and decolonial signs in everyday life, other pedagogies can be identified that are powerful for developing curricular discussions in the area of art/education in peripheral school spaces.

---

[4] The "decolonial option" can be seen as a set of projects that aim to understand and act in a world marked by the permanence of global coloniality at different levels of personal and collective life

From there, following the logic of post-colonial and decolonial studies, four axes of analysis were considered to guide this research: 1) Addressing difference and indenitarian constructions; 2) Challenging the modern artistic canon; 3) Dialogue with local cultural and aesthetic productions. The axes of analysis guiding this research - formulated on the basis of perceptions of how the teachers surveyed deal with problems and possibilities similar to those I am proposing, and also on the basis of the readings carried out - are described below:

According to Marin (2009), "the approach to the relationship between local knowledge and universal knowledge, imposed by the dominant culture, is the main reference for the theoretical proposition of the decolonization of knowledge" (MARIN, 2009, p.1). The author thus argues that the main challenge for education is to start from each reality, based on local cultures and the adaptation of their possibilities.[66] and adapting its possibilities to the global context. Based on this proposition transposed to the field of art/education, the first thematic axis of this research is the identification of possible dialogues between local cultural, aesthetic and artistic productions and the school, establishing fundamental relationships between local knowledge (as a new locus of enunciation) and global knowledge, in terms of cultural and artistic forms and other aesthetic expressions.

According to Mignolo (2003), problematizing colonial difference, identities and identification involved in processes of disengagement from modernity-coloniality are fundamental discussions for the decolonial option because they help to construct other identities, unveiling the hegemonic legitimacy of the "knowledge" intrinsic to modernity, which denies agency and validation to identities that have already been constructed, but which are subalternized. Therefore, reflections on difference, subalternity, new subjectivities, the "Other", etc., are also a set of concerns that make up the second thematic axis of this research.

Decolonial thinkers, especially Mignolo (2003, 2005, 2007, 2012), also reflect on the relationship between
coloniality/decoloniality and aesthetics, from which the term "decolonial aesthetics" was coined[77]. The notion of "decolonial aesthetics" aims to recognize options open to other meanings, other aesthetics that disobey and contest the cognitive and aesthetic codes of modernity. It is therefore about constructing a reflection on the epistemic, ethical and political fields of coloniality-modernity, from the context of an aesthetic decoloniality. In the words of Mignolo (2012,

[6] On the other hand, it is also naive to think that education can be "saved" simply by recognizing the supposed essences of local cultures. Here, the main risk we run is that of reification, guided by a certain neo-colonial culturalism

[7] In November 2010, the academic event "Decolonial Aesthetics" was held at the Faculty of Arts-ASAB of the Universidad Distrital Francisco Jose de Caldas in Bogota, Colombia. With the participation of Walter Mignolo, this event set out to think about the problem of the coloniality/decoloniality of aesthetics, as a questioning of the constituent dimensions of modernity/coloniality.

p.13), a construction "based on particular, local aesthetics and histories that nevertheless point to common horizons in an inhomogeneous diversity of knowledge, know-how and practices". In this sense, I connect the ideas presented in the sense of an aesthetic decoloniality with the arguments of Jagodzinski (2008) who, in the context of curricular production in art/education, proposes a "defiance" and "re-evaluation of Euro-American narcissism" (JAGODZINSKI, 2008, p.684). Following a post-colonial line of thought, this author proposes that the discussion of art/education curricula should introduce a disaffiliatory discourse in relation to the modern artistic canon, "integrating and deconstructing its binarisms. This means identifying the exclusions on which it was founded" (JAGODZINSKI, 2008, p.685), especially the artistic production and aesthetic expressions of subalternized groups. This reading neither removes nor diminishes the importance of canonized art, but introduces a destabilizing element, according to other perspectives. In this sense, the possibilities opened up by the attitude of disaffiliation from the modern-colonial artistic canon and the identification of decolonial aesthetics in art/education become the third articulating axis of this research.

As presented so far, thinking about art/education in peripheral school spaces according to a decolonial logic, taking into account other rationalities, is the main purpose of this research. In this sense, it is necessary to incorporate the contexts and subjects that make up these spaces from a critical position on culture, highlighting power relations and introducing dissent in relation to the canonized art inherited from modernity. However, in order to move towards a decolonizing art/education, it is necessary to be aware that emancipatory projects are under construction in "a future of plural and concrete possibilities, simultaneously utopian and realistic, which are being built in the present" (SANTOS, 2004, p.254).

In this sense, it is essential to carefully observe the spaces open to the diversity of uses and experiences in the plurality and unpredictability of everyday school life. This means recognizing the emancipatory and decolonial possibilities invented on a daily basis, which make it possible to establish a (re)appropriation of the pedagogical space as a practiced place (CERTEAU, 2008) and ensure the active dimension of subjects in the production of knowledge and social practices. According to this perspective, it is necessary to be willing to learn from what is emerging, from what is happening and not just from what is established and recognized in art/education, including the space for improvisation, for mistakes, for what is not fully realized and for ideas that fall by the wayside. It is in this sense that the paths towards a decolonial pedagogy in art/education encompass the unpredictability and plurality of everyday life, making it possible to open up to other aesthetics, other logics and other thoughts, valuing the pluriversality of existing epistemes and types of knowledge.

1 PREDOMINANT NARRATIVES IN EDUCATION

The things we take for granted, without questioning them or reflecting on them, are the very things that determine our conscious thought and decide our conclusions.

John Dewey

The function for which the school was institutionalized, since the 19th century, as a moulder of identities, a transmitter of watertight knowledge and sustained by the reproduction of social stratification, remains almost intact, despite its agony, and despite the distance between what the school offers and the expectations and experiences of the students. In this scenario, there are successive narratives that are naturalized in school education, such as those that defend citizenship as the basic function of the school, a narrative that emanates from the Enlightenment, later adapted to democratic practice in post-industrial societies. We also often come across a narrative that appeals to the idea that education must adapt to the demands of the market, mediated by the needs and dictates of the production system.

In this logic, education is evaluated in tests carried out to measure the effectiveness of the education system. In the case of Brazil, competency tests such as the "Prova Brasil" and the Basic Education Assessment System (SAEB), which rank schools according to the Basic Education Development Index (IDEB), are examples of this trend. These narratives succeed each other and coexist with their variants without, however, responding to the needs of the subjects present in schools, especially in the case of public and peripheral school spaces. As Hernandez (2007, p.13) points out, the predominant narrative in our schools is the one generated by European colonization since the 16th century:

> One of the results of this narrative is the construction of a vision of 'us' and 'others' determined by the hegemony of white, Christian and Western (European and now North American) men. This narrative is projected in the selection of some school knowledge in which the "other" (the one who is not part of the hegemonic "us") is presented in a subordinate position. - In this way, the "other" (the one who is not part of the hegemonic "us") is presented in a subordinate position, whereby he has to be civilized and therefore justifiably exploited and stripped of his knowledge. This is why, to a large extent, the school's view of knowledge is mediated by the idea of cultural domination, which makes us see/treat the other as subordinate. This other would be boys, girls (children) and young people and, in part, teachers and families (HERNANDEZ 2007, p.13).

As far as the Brazilian reality is concerned, educational policies and reforms have adapted and responded to economic policies, determining an economistic and highly efficient approach to education, subordinating it to the logic of the market. Consistent with the World Bank's guidelines, a series of measures aimed at making education more competitive, more productive and more in tune with the demands of companies and industries have been taken. Among them is the adoption of proposals that emphasize the centralized control of the curriculum through the National Curriculum Parameters (PCNs) and the association of the curriculum with a national evaluation system. These educational reforms correspond to international trends that involve the mobilization of resources to hire teams of notables (from outside the schools) to define official knowledge through curricular documents that are received and applied *from the top down* (MACEDO and MOREIRA, 2001, p.15), which puts into the background interactions and movements that take place at the micro level.

Through this process of subordination to international trends and the logic of the market, the responsibility for finding solutions to the problems of a highly exclusive society is projected onto education. According to Candau (2001, p.34),

> We are thus experiencing a strong contradiction between the discourse that formally values education and prioritizes basic schooling for all and the real situation of many schools and the working conditions of teachers in the public system. These are presented as inefficient and resistant to the proposed changes (CANDAU, 2001 p.34).

Another important aspect of this discussion concerns the emphasis of neoliberal precepts in the organization of school work and the incoherence of the hegemonic discourse on "education for diversity". The reforms are based on the arguments of psychopedagogy, which points to individual differences as something to be taken into account and even encouraged in the teaching-learning process. It is differences in knowledge, with an emphasis on meritocratic aspects, that support the idea that qualities are innate. The political aspect of the differences is not taken into account, since the emphasis on the "score" presupposes behaviors and capacities that would be located in the individual.

This situation highlights another basic contradiction in the educational and curricular discourse, which "values differences" and "respects diversity", when it institutes a highly exclusionary project for society, which has competition and individualism as its fundamental anchors. Pursuing a common curricular standard as a way of promoting an "inclusive" educational policy for subordinate groups (the Others of modernity) turns out to be perversely mistaken, insofar as educational issues linked to differences and processes of identification are issues that originate in other processes involving the creation of new meanings in the environment regulated by hegemonic discursive systems.

In this way, the assimilation of difference through education, conceived as a "civilizing mission", a characteristic inherited from colonialism, is being questioned and is giving rise to other movements to reinvent the school. In this sense, LOPES (2001, p. 75) emphasizes the commitment to

> [...] criticism of the processes of homogenization and hierarchization of cultures, considering cultural plurality at the level of rationality. Incorporating this perspective into the school curriculum requires transforming not only the content and methods taught, but also the epistemological and sociological principles by which knowledge is constructed and interpreted. It also requires that we stop conceiving of knowledge as ready-made, finished, neutral, without a historical character, without the marks of class and interests (LOPES, 2001, p. 75).

In school education, knowledge has been signified and legitimized "by efficiently serving certain ends, without problematizing the processes that lead to these ends" (LOPES and MACEDO, 2011 p.73), from an instrumental perspective. Knowledge becomes a mere auxiliary instrument of the economic process, as it is used as a universal tool to serve this purpose. In this technical-instrumental process, "the subject is reified, its consciousness is extirpated and it does not participate in the process of rational signification" (LOPES and MACEDO, 201, p.74).

According to Boaventura de Souza Santos (2004b), today we are experiencing a paradigmatic crisis with the questioning of the unified and universalizing categories of Western modernity, which conceives of scientific knowledge (academic and instrumental) as the only one considered valid. This questioning has consequences for the debate about which knowledge should be included in the curriculum and, consequently, which should be excluded. However, there are enormous difficulties in changing the dominant narrative (technical-instrumental/modern colonial) which tends towards naturalization: "things are as they are and cannot be thought of in any other way". This line of thinking is perpetuated through what Santos (2004) calls indolent reason, characterized by acting from reductionist categories and by not trying hard enough to recognize the infinite epistemological diversity present in other ways of producing knowledge.

1.1 Indolent reason doesn't want to bother thinking

According to Santos (2004), indolent reason is a model of Western rationality that reproduces ways of thinking that perpetuate exclusionary practices, because it does not consider social experiences to be relevant. One of the ways in which indolent reasoning takes place is through the idea that "what is in place cannot be fought for" and therefore cannot be changed. Indolent reason doesn't feel the need to learn more, it considers itself to know everything, so it doesn't need to change or show that it can change; on the contrary, it sees its rationality as unique and absolute, disregarding any counter-hegemonic alternative.

Although we come into contact with alternative experiences through different instituting practices, these do not significantly affect the dominance of the dominant rationality model.

> There has been no restructuring of knowledge. Nor could there have been, in my opinion, because the indolence of reason manifests itself, among other things, in the way it resists changing routines and transforms hegemonic interests into true knowledge. (SANTOS, 2004, p. 6)

In order to understand how these models of thought are naturalized in education, we used the notion of *"hybris of the zero point"* coined by Castro-Gomez (2005) which, in turn, is connected to the concepts of coloniality of power and knowledge (LANDER, 2005; QUIJANO, 2007; MIGNOLO, 2008; GROSFOGUEL, 2008). The "zero point" is a starting point of observation, supposedly neutral and absolute, in which scientific language since the Enlightenment assumes itself to be "the most perfect of all human languages" and which reflects "the purest universal structure of reason" (CASTRO-GOMEZ, 2005c, p. 14). The logic of the "zero point" is Eurocentric and "presumes the totalization of Western gnosis, founded on Greek, Latin and the six modern European imperial languages" (MIGNOLO, 2008, p. 29). It founds and sustains modern colonial rationality:

> It is, then, a philosophy in which the epistemic subject has no sexuality, gender, ethnicity, race, class, spirituality, language, or epistemic location in any relation of power, [...] and produces truth from an inner monologue with itself, without relation to anyone outside itself. In other words, it is a deaf philosophy, without a face and without a force of gravity. The faceless subject floats through the sky without being determined by anything or anyone [...]. It will be taken up by the human sciences from the 19th century onwards as the epistemology of axiological neutrality and the empirical objectivity of the subject who produces scientific knowledge (GROSFOGUEL, 2008, p. 64-65).

This model of thought, reproduced in an uncontested way, is linked to the concept of the coloniality of power and, more specifically, the coloniality of knowledge. The concept of coloniality of power denounces "the continuity of colonial forms of domination after the end of colonial administrations, produced by colonial cultures and the structures of the modern-colonial capitalist world-system" (GROSFOGUEL, 2008, p.126). For Mignolo (2003), Western expansion after the 16th century was not only economic and religious, but also of hegemonic forms of knowledge, of a concept of representation of knowledge and cognition, imposing itself as epistemic, political and historiographical hegemony, thus establishing the coloniality of knowledge. Intrinsically linked to the coloniality of power, the coloniality of knowledge points to the epistemological legacy of Eurocentrism, which prevents us from understanding the world from other epistemes.

During my day-to-day monitoring of art classes at Mauro de Castro Secondary School, in addition to art classes, I also went to the teachers' room during breaks. There I heard conversations, which wouldn't be very different in other schools, from some fellow teachers who complained about the students being disrespectful and undisciplined. However, as this is a school next to the largest landfill in Latin America, in a community linked to the recycling of materials, the following statements are striking: "The children have to be recycled!", "These students, they don't speak properly, they don't walk properly, they don't eat properly, they don't sit properly...". Apparently, the frustration of some teachers stems from the fact that their students from the periphery stubbornly do not fit into the models of behavior and education considered ideal.

In this way, from the civilizing tradition of modernity, models of thought and ideas that have been considered true are reproduced, which give continuity to the asymmetrical power relations that have been established, and which continue to serve as the basis for educational ideas, as well as educational policies. Seeking change seems utopian, unrealistic, because everything is reproduced or merely adapted, there is no paradigm shift, as if another way of living were not possible. However, in the school space, thoughts coexist that have learned to live between different logics, to move between different codes and that do not fit into the modern parameters of observation, control and formal organization of concrete reality.

1.2 Another perspective, from the margins.

In the epistemological debate, Santos (2006) states that what he calls the sociology of emergencies confronts the previously debated indolent reason. According to the author, this sociology of emergencies promotes a symbolic amplification of a small social movement, a small collective action, without discrediting its potential for change due to its potential reach. The sociology of emergencies produces

> [...] possible experiences, which are not given because there are no alternatives, but are possible and already exist as an emergency. [...] It's not about an abstract future, but the future of which we have clues and signs [...]. The sociology of emergencies is what allows us to abandon the idea of an unlimited future and replace it with a concrete future. (SANTOS, 2006, p. 31).

The neoliberal capitalist world based on growing competitiveness and the negation of the other reproduces what Santos (2004) calls the "waste of experience". According to the author, "social experience around the world is much broader and more varied than what the Western scientific or philosophical tradition knows and considers important" (SANTOS, 2004, p.2). This process establishes a subalternizing distinction from other forms of knowledge.

In order to change this situation, Santos proposes adopting another perspective, from the margins, from the most extreme peripheries of Western modernity, in order to create a new critical gaze that allows us to question who produces knowledge, in what context and for whom. This look from the margins, in the context of schools in peripheral regions, seeks to value the specificity of different educational *spaces and times*, demanding that these practices be local in order to be legitimate (OLIVEIRA 2012).

In this sense, Santos (1995) points out that "the more global the problems, the more local the solutions", understanding that these follow local mini-rationalities. In this sense, it is through the development of radically local social practices that other educational practices gain their political meaning. These practices, many already in development, exist and need to be recognized in their political and epistemological *status*.

The situations experienced at E.M. Mauro de Castro exemplify difficulties in developing other practices, but also some possibilities. On one occasion, the 8th graders organized a birthday party for their teacher Mariane in the classroom. Someone said: "Aren't you going to play music?". A stereo was then improvised, playing bass and songs of the young people's choice. It didn't take long for someone from the school administration to arrive and say: "No, funk is not allowed!". The sound was turned off. Unlike this kind of attitude, on another day, during an art lesson for the same class, teacher Mariane suggested that they do a rereading of the "Venus de Milo", deliberately changing some aspects of the original figure. Then, a group of boys wanted to put their arms back on the Venus de Milo, holding rifles. The teacher's reaction shows her position as an educator:

> Teacher - Rifles? Great! But let's think: what is a rifle?

> Student: Oh, and a gun.
> Teacher - Why do you want to draw the gun? Let's think about it. Student - I don't know, it's cool.
> Teacher - Why is it cool? Who has the gun?
> Student - Whoever has a gun has power, has power in the situation.
> Teacher: Ah, so what you want to draw is a symbol of power! Is it only a gun that brings that? What does it mean to have power for those of us who live on the outskirts?

In the end, the students drew the picture with guns, but the most important thing was that this was not done without problematizing their intentions, based on the teacher's reflective intervention. From this, we can understand that what already exists can be revised and replaced when the needs and purposes of education change. Plurality is important as opposed to homogenization.

Taking this position means moving away from strategies that invite us to maintain the modern discourse, which reinforce the current forms of domination over subalternized cultures, contributing to the maintenance of the colonial matrix of power (MIGNOLO, 2003). This position goes in a different direction from those who move forward with prioritization agendas focused on stable achievements, on accommodating education to the logic of homogenization or on diluting the implication of differences through the discourse of valuing diversity. These are currently hegemonic practices that do not meet people's needs to make sense of the world in which they live and their own experiences. By considering other pedagogical practices, it becomes possible to identify ways to break the hegemonic pattern of thinking about education and to break the zero-point epistemology that establishes that reality - school education - cannot be thought beyond the dominant rationality. A zero point that establishes that it is only possible to make partial innovations so that everything remains the same. A zero point that reinforces and values the process of submitting students to forms of learning and assessment based on repetition, on denying the sense of being and the questions that really help them to give meaning to the world in which they live.

1.3 Colonialities in Art History/Education

> ... Only anthropophagy unites us. Socially. Economically [...]. Philosophically. We were never catechized. It was Carnival. The Indian dressed up as a senator from the Empire. Pretending to be Pitt. Or appearing in the works of Alencar full of Portuguese good feelings [...]. Before the Portuguese discovered Brazil, Brazil had discovered happiness. [...] Our independence has not yet been proclaimed. Typical phrase of King João VI: - My son, put that crown on your head before some adventurer does! We expelled the

> dynasty. We must expel the Bragantine spirit, the ordinances and the rape of Maria da Fonte (ANDRADE, 1970, p. 13-19).

Despite Oswald de Andrade's manifesto, which already at the beginning of the 20th century was in favour of a decolonizing attitude through the metaphor of anthropophagy, evoking an intellectual stance of appropriating (swallowing) ideas from abroad, with regard to art teaching in Brazil, it can be said that it originated in the context of colonialism, characterized by cultural dependence and the import of foreign models (BARBOSA and COUTINHO, 2011). In this same sense, the teaching of arts in Brazilian schools remains deeply marked by multiple facets of coloniality in the relations of knowledge and power. Considering Brazil's colonial origins, we can say, based on Duarte (2007, p.120), that "the colonizers never intended to allow the development of the arts.

a culture with its own characteristics". The result was the importation of European culture to serve the interests of the ruling class, which repressed the development of values and meanings of local cultural life.

In this context, the first institutionalization of art teaching was the French Mission (1816) with its neoclassical model, which was imported to Brazil. With the arrival of the court in Brazil at the beginning of the 19th century, national culture had to be modernized. In order to officially start teaching the arts, French artists were brought in to form the so-called French Mission. Through it, the Academy of Fine Arts was founded, considered to be the beginning of artistic education in Brazil.

However, the teaching brought by the French also proved to be an imposition of values and a cultural invasion of an elitist nature (BARBOSA and COUTINHO, 2011). In Brazil, the Baroque style - also brought from abroad - had been popularized, slowly assimilated, already expressing local characteristics, and what was brought by the French Mission was the Neoclassical style, which at the time was a novelty in Europe. The Brazilian elites, adhering to the "modern", rejected the Baroque, considering it to be in bad taste. "A class prejudice based on aesthetic categorization was installed". (BARBOSA, p.31, 1995). This is the origin of one of the greatest prejudices against art that persists to this day: by distancing art from popular contact, the idea of art as a superfluous activity, a "cultural drivel" (BARBOSA, p.41, 1984) that was of no interest to daily life, was generated among us. The perspective of the educational activity of the Imperial School of Fine Arts then became the place of convergence of a cultural elite that was being formed in the country to move the court, thus hindering the access of the lower classes to artistic production. In this way, the Imperial School of Fine Arts inaugurated the ambiguity in which Brazilian education is still debated today, that is, the dichotomy between elite education and popular education.

Until 1870, there was little challenge to the art teaching model of the Imperial Academy of Fine Arts, which was partly used by secondary schools.

> In private secondary schools for boys and girls, there was a prevalence of copying portraits of important people and saints and copying European prints depicting landscapes unknown to our eyes, which were accustomed to the tropical environment. These landscapes led students to value European nature aesthetically and to depreciate ours for its contrasting coarseness (BARBOSA and COUTINHO, p.8, 2011).

It's interesting to note that in the 19th century few New World countries instituted art teaching for boys in elite schools. Most commonly, art was only taught in schools for upper-class girls. In Brazil, this was because the Brazilian elite was more closely linked to aristocratic models during the colonial period than to bourgeois models as in other American countries.

According to the aristocratic model, art was indispensable in the education of princes. King João VI set an example when he hired a private teacher to teach drawing to the princes. Following this model, art was included in 1811 in the curriculum of Father Felisberto Antonio Figueiredo de Moura's school, a boys' school in Rio de Janeiro that set the model for education for upper-class boys at the time.

Today, it is neither strange nor incomprehensible to hear that "Art is an elitist thing". This was said by a math teacher in the teachers' room of the Mauro de Castro Secondary School in Duque de Caxias in November 2014. The teacher wanted the art teacher to teach the students how to draw geometric shapes because it would help them learn the mathematics content. According to him, mathematics is important because *"it's how the school is evaluated"*.

The art teacher was not very comfortable, and resisted the idea of teaching geometric shapes based on these arguments. This was followed by a discussion about the function and usefulness of school subjects, when the teacher expressed among his arguments that *"Art is an elitist thing, it's made to be seen only by those who 'understand' in closed groups, those who don't understand are left out, they don't even want to know what it is"*.

Leaving aside the discussion about the greater or lesser importance occupied by a given subject in the school curriculum, the math teacher has every reason to perceive art as something elitist. After all, art as cultural adornment is a founding conception of art teaching in Brazil and a colonial trait that remains even today.

From 1870 onwards, opposed to teaching art exclusively in schools for the elite, some liberals, with the creation of the Republican party, defended the idea that popular education for work should be the main objective of art in school and began a campaign to make drawing (especially geometric drawing) compulsory in primary and secondary education, on the grounds of educating the nation for industrial work. In this way, the model of teaching drawing applied to industry developed for the American educational system was imported and began to be disseminated in Brazil by figures such as Rui Barbosa, who endorsed the American conceptions of the teaching of drawing in his opinions for the reform of the Brazilian educational system[810].

Rui Barbosa's guidelines for teaching drawing in Brazilian gymnasiums became official through the educational reform of 1901. From then on, its contents, which had already entered the circuit of Brazilian education, remained almost unchanged until 1958, going through several educational reforms and there are still remnants of them in art classes.

In practice, the gap between art education for the elite and the working classes was exacerbated. Thus, the children of the upper classes had art appreciation classes in their schools and learned to copy reproductions of famous works of art in the sense of cultural elevation, while the children of workers were prepared for work in the factories through geometric drawing and linear drawing.

In schools, in addition to the objective of educating the working class for the job market, the teaching of drawing was defended by modern-colonial evolutionist ideas, such as the purpose of developing knowledge through the study and copying of ornaments, as these represented the imaginative strength of man in his evolution from primitive ages.

> When teaching drawing, it was recommended that one should start with bas-reliefs composed of straight lines, because this composition of ornaments was the most summary and corresponded to the ornamental expression of the primitive peoples of Oceania and Africa, and then move on to the models in curves and capricious lines found in the decoration of more evolved peoples [....] and only then to introduce high-reliefs representing figures of fauna and flora, a more complex expression, characteristic of the Greeks at the beginning of their history. (BARBOSA and COUTINHO, p.14, 2011).

This model of evolutionist thinking, which refers to Greco-Roman culture as the cradle of all knowledge of "evolved" Western culture, has been naturalized and is still very present in education today, based on the Greco-Roman ideological sequence of modern Christian Europe as being unilinear, according to Dussel (1993, p.26), an "ideological invention that abducts Greek culture as exclusively European and Western and pretends that since the Greek and Roman eras these cultures have been the center of world history". This is the notion that founds and sustains modern-colonial racist rationality.

Art teacher Mariane Travassos shows that, in order to build new, decolonial paths, it is necessary to develop a critical understanding of[8] art history: "*If today we work with African history and art, this doesn't exist at the School of Fine Arts (EBA-UFRJ).*" (Art teacher)

Regarding the selection of themes for her art classes according to the Eurocentric model, the teacher says:

> My model, which is the so-called "normal" one, which is Eurocentric culture, makes me select the generating themes. But when I go into the classroom and see all those kids, beautiful, multi-colored, multi-everything, with so much history, there's no way that the class can deny that. They get into the content. That's it. I think I could define my classes like this: the content is transformed by them. I think that's how it has to be. (TRAVASSOS, M. Interview given to Andre Dias Pires. Duque de Caxias, June 10, 2014).

Through her words, the teacher reveals a strong awareness of the socio-cultural origins and existential universe of her students, demonstrating that in her work environment, in a peripheral public school, it is possible to assume a decolonial attitude, seeking to undermine and destabilize modernity from a position outside of it, created from within. I'm referring to the traditional contents of the curriculum under which art teachers are trained, from which coloniality can be problematized.

However, we can say that, from the outset, the educational vision of art teaching was based on multiple swallowings - still poorly digested - and appropriations of external models seeking to reconcile and synthesize diverse and distinct currents of thought, in which European culture continued to be the ideal of civilization and good education. The local reality was never seen through the eyes of our planners. The lower classes, always seen as ignorant and backward, had their education geared towards the production of labor, and art, considered a luxury and interpreted according to European canons, was intended for the education and leisure of the wealthier classes. These classes also never looked kindly on popular artistic manifestations that were considered "primitive" and "uncultured". The people, who had no access to elite art, were also discouraged and even repressed in their aesthetic manifestations.

When art teaching became the subject of discussion again in 1927, the idea was to modernize education. Influenced by the avant-garde movements in European

[8] Opinions on the primary and secondary education reform of 1882

art, children's art came to be seen as having an aesthetic value linked to the spontaneity of the child. The same liberal principle of art integrated into the curriculum, or rather, art in school for all, was defended. However, while the liberals aimed to teach the technical aspects of drawing to prepare for work, the modernists represented through the movement known as the "new school" defended the idea of art as an instrument that mobilizes emotional liberation, based on self-expression and individual freedom.

The vision of the individual that predominated during this period was linked to a conception of the transformative power of art and creative spontaneity that coincided with the triumph of the Allies in the Second World War, and the promotion of values about individual freedoms. However, in Brazil, the libertarian impetus of the Scholastic ideas, in the sense of art as the emotional liberation of the individual, was soon interrupted by the new state. Some procedures that had already been tried out in Brazilian education were consolidated, such as geometric drawing in secondary and primary schools, pedagogical drawing and the copying of prints used for Portuguese composition classes. This is the beginning of the pedagogization of art at school. From then on, we will see an emptied use of art in school, used in an instrumental sense to train the eye and vision or in a vague and imprecise sense of emotional liberation and for the development of values typical of modernity such as avant-garde originality and creativity, the latter considered as beauty or novelty.

Since the dictatorship in 1964, art in public primary schools has generally been dominated by suggested themes and drawings alluding to civic, religious and other celebrations. By 1969, art was part of the curriculum in all prestigious private schools, following the methodological line of varying techniques. However, there were very few public schools that did any art work.

In 1971, the Law of Guidelines and Bases of National Education (LDB) included art in the school curriculum under the title of Art Education, but it was considered an "educational activity" and not a subject. In ordinary public secondary schools, geometric drawing continued to predominate, with content almost identical to that found in the educational reform of 1901, in addition to the aforementioned use of the arts subject in festivals and civic celebrations. Barbosa and Coutinho (2011) cite a passage that draws attention to art in education during this period:

> Sao Paulo was under the rule of a right-wing politician, Paulo Maluf, who suggested that art teachers spend the year training their students to sing a few songs to be performed in a choir of ten thousand children, accompanied by him on the piano, in a soccer stadium at Christmas. As a reward, teachers

> who prepared their children would get five points towards a teaching career, whereas a master's degree was worth ten points (BARBOSA; COUTINHO, 2011).

A new reflection on art/education linked to the specificity of art was only realized in the 1980s with the dissemination of research carried out by Ana Mae Barbosa through what became known as the Triangular Proposal, based on three axes: making art, reading the work of art, and historical contextualization. According to Barbosa and Coutinho (2011), "The Triangular Proposal was characterized by the entry of the image, its decoding and interpretation into the classroom along with the already achieved expressiveness".

When art became a compulsory subject in basic education in the 1990s (LDB/1996) and the National Curriculum Parameters were established, the Triangular Proposal was taken as a guideline for the art area, although not explicitly. Despite some distortions, the ideas of the Triangular Proposal represent a significant advance for Brazilian art/education, forming part of a contemporary trend that conceives of art not as standardized knowledge, nor as inner expression, but as a cultural fact.

In this sense, we are currently participating in an intense debate on the relevance of rethinking conceptual and methodological changes that presuppose a change in the purpose of art in school education, since it "considers the insertion of subjects in the cultural environment and the transits and exchanges in various contexts" (BARBOSA and COUTINHO, 2011, p.49). In this process, the educational proposals coming from visual culture studies are becoming increasingly influential in the debates on art/education in Brazil.

Formulated from cultural studies in England and North America in the second half of the 20th century, the proposal of education for visual culture introduces, according to Aguirre (2011, p.77), art and art education into a convulsive process of changing paradigms in relation to the aesthetic regime of modernity. In reality, this debate reflects a moment in which we can distinguish a number of factors. On the one hand, we have the failure of modernity's aesthetic utopia and the consequent loss of hope in art's ability to contribute to a transformation of collective living conditions. On the other hand, with the expansion of the idea of art in the face of the diversification of the field of artistic practices, art studies have found themselves faced with paradoxes that have led them to question, for example, the analogies and differences between the canonical arts and visual culture, between theater and the dramaturgical productions of the mass media, or the legitimacy and hegemony of cultured art forms in relation to popular forms. As well as the displacement of the aesthetic from the realm of the arts to all corners of everyday life.

In the proposal of Visual Culture Studies, the theoretical and didactic foundations of visual arts teaching are necessarily revised. It is necessary to think of the visual in terms of cultural meaning, social practices and power relations. It is necessary to reflect on ways of looking and producing looks. It presupposes a radical change from the study of art to the study of visual culture, a change in the object of study and content.

These new contexts influence the debates and practices of art/education in Brazil, opening up new fields of inquiry for decolonial criticism by demanding consideration of the role of images in the production and reproduction of "colonial difference" (MIGNOLO 2003). In this way, various studies have been initiated that question artistic disciplines and the regime of the gaze from the concepts proposed by decolonial criticism. However, we should carefully consider the critique made by Cristian Leon (2012, p.2) suggesting that "one of the outstanding challenges for visuality studies is the critique of the underlying universalism hidden behind the term visual culture". This universalist myth of modernity prevents us from thinking about "geographical, spiritual, ethnic and linguistic hierarchies, as well as those of class, gender, race and nation" (LEON, 2012, p.2). In this way, the debates proposed for rethinking art/education in contemporary times, including decolonial thinking, are called upon to reintroduce and represent the geographical and epistemological discontinuity surrounding art and aesthetic expressions.

2 AESTHETICS AND THE DECOLONIAL OPTION

What kind of aesthetics does a subject need (if any) who cannot or does not want to subscribe to modern aesthetics because of his partial belonging to Western modernity, or his radical non-belonging to it?

Madina Tlostanova

Aesthetics and art are more a matter of politics than anything else.

Susette Min

In a certain sense, aesthetics and decoloniality are in an asymmetrical relationship with each other. Initially, aesthetics is commonly seen as a (white) colonial discourse of the "autonomy of art", always reaffirming historically and, in the present, its white, heteronormative and Western genealogy. Precisely because of this genealogy, art seems to develop in a depoliticized field, which keeps aesthetic legitimacy completely separate from social legitimacy.

However, on the other hand, Ranciere (2005) ponders that it is in the distribution of access to material and symbolic space and in the configuration of the regime of division of the sensible that the aesthetic and the artistic are allied to the political. In this way, the political, in relation to art, can be understood as the game of decisions about what can be seen and said, about who has the competence, the quality to see and to say or about what the properties of the spaces of seeing and saying are and the characteristics of access to them.

According to this conception, it is therefore necessary to re-politicize the relationships established between aesthetics, art and politics, assuming that aesthetics and art are first and foremost matters of politics. In this sense, decolonial criticism has made important advances and considerations that can constitute a relevant epistemological tool for thinking about the space of aesthetic experiences beyond modern coloniality. Decolonial authors such as Gomez and Mignolo (2012) have broadened their reflexive and critical approach to the epistemic, ethical and political context of modernity/coloniality to include, specifically, the proposition of aesthetic decoloniality.

In this sense, these authors try to build general lines for this approach, in search of decolonial options from the horizon of senses and meanings produced from aesthetic-others and "particular, localized histories" produced in the context of subalternized cultures (MIGNOLO, 2012, p.13). These represent singular experiences which, however, point to a common ground in a pluriversality of knowledge, skills and practices (MIGNOLO, 2005).

In their conceptualization of aesthetics and the decolonial option, Gomez and Mignolo (2012) highlight aspects of artistic production and connect them in a discourse aimed at the public interested in art, as well as teachers and students, which aims to offer tools for "feeling and thinking" about art.

Regarding aesthetic decoloniality, the authors state that,

> It is a search, not an enclosure in the house of the Western being, but a stay in one's own house; it is a search for one's own self, on whose path one dismantles everything that covers it up, deodorizes it, silences it and deforms it. [...Here, elements of macro-structural analysis - such as the colonial matrix of power, the world-system, geopolitics, global phenomena - are crossed with singular practical issues of art and culture, Aesthetics and the decolonial option are localized histories that are also embodied (body-litique), through power relations, in the cultural space as an ideological battlefield where the struggle for decoloniality is won or lost (GOMEZ, MIGNOLO, 2012, p. 12).

In this way, the decolonial dimension of aesthetics is of great importance alongside the decoloniality of knowledge and being. Decolonial thinking and doing begins with the very concept of coloniality and the colonial pattern of power. This pattern, as decolonial authors point out, has various spheres: political, economic and epistemic. According to Mignolo (2012), the epistemic dimension is the most important, since it regulates and defines the political and the economic. According to the author, neither the political nor the economic has a proper existence in the colonial matrix of power without epistemic regulation, while the epistemic also regulates the spheres of gender and sexuality, racial classification, knowledge and aesthetics. According to Mignolo (2012), in this sense, the epistemic has a double role: that of controller and protagonist. As a protagonist, the epistemic is part of the sphere of knowledge and the distinction between knowing and feeling, between reason and feelings, between rationality and aesthetics. As a controller, it is in the epistemic of Western cosmology where all these distinctions make sense, coloniality is maintained and updated. This is why it is necessary to detach ourselves, as Quijano (2005) insists, from Eurocentrism as an epistemological issue.

Mignolo (2012) argues that the time has come for aesthetics to detach itself from this Eurocentrism. In this sense, the author undertakes an analysis of the historical construction of the concept of "aesthetics" derived from "aisthesis".

Aisthesis has its origins in Ancient Greek and its meanings lie around terms such as "sensation", "process of perception". However, from the 17th century onwards, the concept of aisthesis was linked to the concept of "the sensation of beauty", giving rise to "aesthetics" as a theory whose practice would be "art". According to Mignolo, this operation represented the colonization of aisthesis by aesthetics, since, if aisthesis is a phenomenon possible for all human beings, aesthetics would only be a particular theory of such sensations as a function of beauty. In other words, there is no universal law that relates aisthesis to beauty; this relationship is a construction, just as the concept of beauty itself is. Thus, from the moment that aisthesis is related to the idea of beauty (which is claimed to be a universal truth), we rule out any possibility that a different aesthetic experience could occur at a time before or in a space outside of modernity-coloniality. Therefore, it can be concluded that if aesthetics was constituted as a philosophical discourse in Europe (not in Asia, Africa or Latin America), this discourse contributed, directly and indirectly, to devaluing and therefore "colonizing expressions of feeling and affection" (MIGNOLO, 2012, p.28) in contemporary non-Western societies. According to Mignolo, "All that which does not conform to the rules of taste and rationality - ideally conceived - belongs to the barbarism that must be civilized or to the tradition that must be modernized" (MIGNOLO, 2012, p.38).

In this way, decolonial aesthetics is oriented towards valuing the pluriversality of knowledge, skills and expressive practices, having its point of origin and its trajectory drawn from "the ex-tercer mundo" (MIGNOLO, 2012, p.39). Decolonial aesthetics has its theoretical discourse based on the critical analysis of the control of subjectivity carried out by modern aesthetic art and philosophy (and its derivatives, such as postmodern aesthetics) and manifests itself in expressions of other aesthetics, which have in common the questioning of coloniality and the affirmation of their local identities. Thus, the discourse of decolonial aesthetics "connects the sensibilities and politics of people outside the radio of Western Europe and the United States." (MIGNOLO, 2012, p.39). In this sense, Mignolo (2012) proposes thinking about the decolonization of aesthetics in order to liberate aisthesis. In the author's words,

> To decolonize aesthetics in order to liberate aesthesis, means to disengage from these rules that I bring Kant, because when we read *Observations on the Beautiful and the Sublime* today, it is evident how this reflection on aesthetics is laden with a racism that decalifies the aesthesis of most of the planet. (MIGNOLO, 2012, p.40)

We can understand that decolonizing aesthetics in order to liberate aisthesis means getting rid of continuing to think and do according to modern ideas that are ingrained in the art world, such as the anxiety for the new or novelty, to the detriment of the "old", linked to the sense of tradition or the myth of the solitary and individualistic artist to the detriment of collective forms of aesthetic experience.

2.1 Decolonial Critique of Visuality

What you conceive is what you see; but
what is conceived and what is invented.

Martin Heidegger

Visual culture studies as an educational proposal that has been influencing art/education in the Brazilian school context can also benefit from the studies carried out by decolonial criticism. In this sense, important contributions are being made to thinking about the relationship between power and visuality. According to Leon (2012),

> We could say that one of the effects of the colonization of power and knowledge has been the assimilation of the multiplicity of visual cultures into the binary order of Eurocentrism, which assigns hegemonic and subordinate places to each of them (LEON, 2012, p.115).

In line with the discussion started earlier, there is a pressing need to detach ourselves from theories of art constructed under the parameters of Eurocentric reason, in order to open up to an aesthetic-other of visual cultures-other, as well as an art/education-other. While this is not happening, the tradition handed down from the universal history of art, aesthetics and disciplinary theories of art, remains unquestioned and

continues to be the center for organizing programs and curricula in Fine Arts and Visual Arts in general.

The epistemological detachment and decolonial openness advocated by Mignolo (2012) discusses precisely the effect of questioning Eurocentric categories in order to be able to articulate a way of thinking that enables a place of enunciation for those subjects and histories that have been silenced by Eurocentrism. This line of thought addresses the very constitution of these fields of knowledge in relation to the emergence of modernity-coloniality. In this way, it is open to inter-epistemic dialogue with other knowledges, images and visualities produced by subaltern movements, groups and cultures that express themselves outside the established institutions that authorize what should be art, knowledge, etc.

This context opens up new fields of inquiry for decolonial critique by demanding consideration of the role of images in the production and reproduction of colonial difference and addressing the geopolitical analysis of the role played by devices, institutions (such as schools) and knowledge of art and images in the reproduction of the coloniality of power. According to Leon (2012), there is in fact "a marked hierarchy between Western and non-Western visual systems triggered by a series of technological, iconographic, psychological and cultural mechanisms integrated into colonial systems of power and knowledge" (LEON, 2012, p.115). According to the author, the notion of image also needs to be decolonized, "since it is a product of the optical reticule, the Renaissance perspective, the Western concept of representation and the modern transcendental subject" (LEON, 2012, p.115).

In this way, a powerful universe of categories is structured that transform difference into hierarchy. Languages, gaze codes and visuality also intersect with the other hierarchical orders of modernity-coloniality and serve as parameters for the racialization and inferiorization of non-European populations. Therefore, we could say that one of the effects of the colonization of power and knowledge has been the assimilation of the multiplicity of visual cultures into the binary order of Eurocentrism, which assigns hegemonic and subaltern places to each of them. Furthermore, it can be argued that, in the context of modernity-coloniality, visual cultures that have been racialized and inferiorized through multiple and combined discriminations and hierarchies end up losing their capacity to signify, becoming a pure object of meaning.

In this sense, Joaquin Barriendos (2011) has developed the concept of "coloniality of seeing" to designate the complex intertwining between ethnocentric logic and the technologies of representation and ordering of the gaze produced from the visual regimes inaugurated by modernity-coloniality with the conquest of America.

For the author, the coloniality of seeing is produced by the confluence of the transatlantic expansionism of imperial visual cultures, military-cartographic ocularcentrism, visual rhetoric about Indian cannibalism, the geoepistemic function of imperial cartographies, and the transatlantic symbolic economies that emerged in the sixteenth century (BARRIENDOS, 2011). When these factors come together, a complex visual epistemology is produced that structures, "on the one hand, an order of disembodiment and invisibility that allows the universalization of the imperial gaze and, on the other, an order of embodiment and visibility that allows the racialization of the indigenous body" (LEON, 2012 p.116). Later, this same logic would allow for the inferiorization of women and black people or the sexualization of homosexuals. A kind of moral separation from the other, based on their definition as apolitical beings, outside the laws of men and the laws of God. Inaugurated in modern-coloniality and designed to set in motion its capacity to make other epistemes invisible. According to Barriendos (2011),

> The modern/colonial world-system has given way, then, to the permanent heterogeneous reinvention of a luminous regime which, cyclically, produces and devours the Other, on the one hand, and seeks and hides the mysticism of the beholder, on the other. The *ethnophagous* matrix of the colonial panoptic gaze, that is, the impulse of Eurocentric visuality to stigmatize other ethnicities, has therefore ceased to be colonial, without ceasing to be part of the coloniality of the power of the gaze17. (BARRIENDOS, 2011, p.24)

According to the author (2011), the permanent interchange of these racializing visual regimes produced from the "invention of the New World" is constitutive of the power matrix through which the coloniality of seeing and epistemological racism operate today. It is for this reason that the coloniality of seeing, as well as the coloniality of power, knowledge and being, is also constitutive of modernity. For the author, the question is,

> The reactivation of those visual regimes and iconographic disciplines which, despite having been generated in the course of the transatlantic commercial battles of early colonial modernity, form part of the transcultural grammars of the latest globalization (BARRIENDOS, 2011, p.15).

This is how the deep imbrication of visuality with hierarchies that are not only geographical, spiritual, ethnic and linguistic, but also racial, class, gender and sexual, is established. By studying the relationship between visual culture and the coloniality of power, which is permanently denied by Eurocentrism and Westernism, it is possible to understand the various hierarchies that are persistently produced and which update the coloniality of seeing.

However, Barriendos (2011) makes an important point about the interculturalist discourses of post-coloniality:

> Recognizing the current state of coloniality of seeing does not, however, call for the strengthening of interculturality as an abstract universal dialogue between equals, nor for the restoration of any kind of shared global visual imaginary, but rather for a better understanding of the epistemological and ontological problems arising from the desire to establish a transparent visual dialogue between different knowledges and cultures. (BARRIENDOS, 2011, p.14)
>
> Through this questioning of the pretension to establish a "transparent" visual dialogue, a "global and shared visual imaginary" which, therefore, does not question the asymmetrical power relations in relation to different knowledges and cultures, the author is criticizing the post-colonial perspective and "its paradigm of monoepistemic intercultural rationality" (BARRIENDOS, 2011, p.26).
>
> Therefore, the study of visual cultures needs to advance in the questioning of the various visual ethnocentrisms, without falling into the trap of operating

from the perspective of interculturalist rationalism, which legitimizes the existence of a kind of transculturally innocent and universally valid optical unconscious (BARRIENDOS, 2011, p.26).

In this way, the very historical-structural heterogeneity of the coloniality of seeing means that the various ethnocentric regimes of the coloniality of seeing must be analyzed and contested, that is, included in the agenda of "a new inter-epistemic visual dialogue", which highlights "the racializing matrix that is at the base of the coloniality of seeing" (BARRIENDOS, 2011, p.24).

This inter-epithetical visual dialog, which Barriendos (2011, p.24) also calls "transcultural visual studies", are defined by the author as those that..:

> 1) who have tried to dismantle the discourse of objectivity and visual truth rooted in the invisibility optic of Eurocentric ethnography; 2) who have moved away from the search for anthropological transparency or acculturation; and 3) who have questioned the epistemological scope of both "participant observation" and "experiential interaction" with otherness, based on the critique of the racializing matrix that underlies the coloniality of seeing (BARRIENDOS, 2011, p. 24).24).

We can understand that transcultural visual studies are interested in questioning the epistemological and ontological remnants derived from the logics of ordering the gaze produced from the visual regimes inaugurated by modernity-coloniality, linked to the "postcolonial crisis of ethnographic authority" and to "the geoepistemological needs of Latin America" (BARRIENDOS, 2011, p.24), in short, those that reveal the ethnocentric genealogy inscribed in the coloniality of seeing.

In this sense, in order to be able to position itself as a decolonial strategy, visual studies need, in addition to recognizing and deepening the field of reflection on the processes of subjection, objectification, inferiorization and outrification that arise from the coloniality of seeing, to collaborate in the process of "transmodern and inter-epistemic" (BARRIENDOS, 2011, p.25) de-invisibilization in relation to other epistemologies and visualities.

The question posed by the decolonial critique for visual culture studies seems to be the reflexive deepening of the power matrix of the Western ethnographic gaze, articulated with the construction of a new inter-epistemic dialogue between Eurocentric visual cultures and visual cultures that have been racially inferior, through the coloniality of seeing. In this sense,

> The recognition of the coloniality of the green could lead us to the "discovery" of adjacent, alternative and contesting scopic paradigms, inscribed -perhaps invisibilized- by the historical development of medernity/celeniality (BARRIENDOS, 2011, p.25).

Due to the effects of historical-structural heterogeneity, visual culture reveals itself as a discontinuous fact articulated within the modern-colonial regime. In this way, multiple visual cultures are recognized, occupying hegemonic and subaltern positions due to the effects of coloniality. By highlighting these processes, decolonial critique applied to visual culture studies can become a powerful strategy for building "an other way of thinking that reinaugurates a new way of thinking from a plurality of geohistorically situated points of enunciation" (LEON, 2012, p.111).

2.2 Knowledge Aisthesis and Art

> The pedagogical ideal of the logician is based on the false assumption that productive logical thinking operates according to the laws of logic and has its epistemological basis in them, because it operates according to them and its results agree with them.
>
> *Herbert Read*

The ambivalent and inextricable connection between aisthesis and epistemology appears in many aesthetic theories, both classical and non-classical, in which art invariably acts as a crossroads between being and cognition. In this way, the problems posed are how to legitimize the knowledge acquired through aesthetic experience, including decolonial experience, in the face of knowledge as it is legitimized in Western modernity, and how decolonial art liberates aisthesis, the very forms of sensitivity and cognition of the human being.

In this debate, we must first consider the paradigm shift in relation to the aesthetic regime of modernity which, on a deeper level, leads to the fundamental problematization of aesthetics and art as Western products and to the diagnosis of the crisis of aesthetics as part of the crisis of modernity. In this sense, the foundations on which the idea of art and the specialized knowledge associated with it have traditionally been based, as well as their academic location, are being questioned.

As examples of this movement, some artists, as well as some community artistic practices, seek trans-modern forms (DUSSEL, 2000, p.29), in the sense of overcoming modernity and its principles, through their aesthetic productions. Iranian artist Siah Armajani is critical of her role as an artist: "Our intention is to remain citizens. We are not interested in the myth created around artists and for artists. What concerns us is the mission, the program and the work itself" (Siah ARMAJANI, 1986, apud CHARREU, 2011, p.122). In the same vein, Brazilian "artist" collectives present in their speeches disaffiliatory positions in relation to the status of art: "What still binds us to Art? Why still use this name?

With what strange fascination does she still beckon to some? Fame, prestige, money, cultural journals, the creative genius?" (ROSAS, 2005). These positions indicate a convulsive process of change in relation to the aesthetic regime of modernity with the disintegration of the notion of art.

> If renouncing "Art" is difficult for some, it is perhaps because they have not yet understood that surrendering to life (or to "reality", as some prefer to call it) does not mean the nullification of the aesthetic. [On the contrary, the "artist" here is the thinker, the creator of action strategies, the architect of acts that will reverberate in this same "reality" (ROSAS, 2005).

In this case, the link between art and life becomes functional and is characterized as an action tactic, as a way of bringing art to the public scene of everyday life. This displacement of the aesthetic from the realm of the arts to everyday life, to a certain extent, disregards the particular and distinctive force of the work of art in the order of the sensible, opening up its field of action beyond the regime of the canonical and hegemonic forms of the arts.

In the opposite direction, Ranciere (2005) draws attention to the advantages of considering art as a form of symbolization, whose specificity does not emanate from its aesthetic characteristics, but from how it is articulated with other symbolic systems in each cultural context. For this author, renouncing this distinction within the aesthetic regime would mean wasting the political and strategic potential that art is capable of mobilizing. In this way, maintaining the specificity of art, giving it some kind of distinction within the aesthetic regime, presents itself as an emancipatory and egalitarian alternative for subalternized groups seeking a place of enunciation. From there, the author advocates redistributing the division of the sensible, allowing those who don't have words or images to have them. It's about making visible what wasn't, so that those who don't have time to be anywhere other than in their work can have access to this "other place" (which in this case would be the place occupied by art).

Perhaps it is irrelevant to determine whether something is art or not, but it is more interesting to discuss when, and under what circumstances of power relations, certain artifacts and expressions were considered aesthetically singular, distinctive, according to certain social uses. For a decolonial option based on the art of aesthetics, it is important to develop aesthetic practices that understand art as a process capable of analyzing forms of coloniality and subsequently restoring the symbolic horizon as a universe of meanings, based on the determination to undo the colonial difference, because otherwise we will continue to classify, label, stereotype and fix the diverse ways of being, living, thinking, feeling and expressing ourselves as processes that uninterruptedly reiterate the subalternization of knowledge, peoples and cultures:

> It was none other than the European aesthetics of secular modernity that colonized aesthesis - the ability to perceive through the senses - as part of its global colonization of being and knowledge, leading to strict formulations of what is beautiful and sublime, good and ugly, to the creation of canonical structures, artistic genealogies, specific taxonomies; cultivating preferences of taste, determining, according to Western whims, the role and function of the artist in society, always optimizing what falls out of this network. (TLOSTANOVA, 2012, p.58-59).

Therefore, one of the most devastating consequences of modernity can be identified in the gnosiological and ontological submission according to which the West determines the norm as the only form of legitimate knowledge, while other peoples and other knowledges continue to be classified as deviations, discarded or subjected to various conventions in order to bring them closer to the Western ideal. According to Tlostanova (2012, p.57),

> The ontological marginalization of non-occidental peoples has been expressed in a specific editing of subjectivity and knowledge, while the crucial sphere of intersection between being and knowledge - art - together with other forms of non-rational, or not exclusively rational, knowledge, have been thrown out of modernity. This is where the most promising models of the decolonization of being and knowledge are formed (TLOSTANOVA, 2012, p.57).

In this passage, the author highlights art as a sphere of intersection between being and knowledge, where there is room, therefore, for a diversity of uses and experiences, not exclusively in terms of rational knowledge, but including knowledge related to the emotional, the affective and the sensitive. Thus, art, or more broadly, the aesthetic experience, becomes a way of liberating knowledge and being through subversion, transgression, resistance, "re-existence" (TLOSTANOVA, 2012, p.58) and the overcoming of modernity and its mechanisms, norms and limitations.

However, there is a risk in the decolonial approach to aesthetics and art of only considering the critical analysis of forms of expression that reproduce and legitimize the colonial matrix. These approaches, although of great importance, are limited to diagnosis and do not, in most cases, propose a significant decolonial option that allows us to think about new ways of understanding art and aesthetic experiences and thus fail to contribute to creating new educational processes capable of favoring a different learning of art and other dimensions of the aesthetic experience as a form of colonial knowledge.

According to Tlostanova (2012, p.58), "Reason alone is not capable of decolonizing the epistemic and existential sphere; neither are emotions alone or sensual experience. Art is what is required for the magical effect of its incarnation in the decolonial gesture". According to Aguirre (2011, p.87), this is why the emotional in relation to education should be conceived together, "as the principle and engine of knowledge"; "as a constituent element in the shaping of the social"; "as a shaping element of (ethical-aesthetic) judgment"; "as a basic element of pleasure and desire". According to the author, working with the aesthetic experience "is fertile ground for the generation of surprising emergencies and emotional ruptures that can become aesthetic and political symbolic ruptures" (AGUIRRE, 2011, p.88).

Therefore, a decolonial pedagogy postulates the opening up of other possible routes of knowledge that include the subject as the fundamental protagonist. The space of aesthetic experience as a form of decolonial knowledge must add "the very experience of being otrified and objectified to decolonial sensibility, education and knowledge" (TLOSTANOVA, 2012, p.64). For the author, this requires "an active rational and emotional effort, a certain type of knowledge and critical thinking tools, an analytical ability to metaphorically link, through art, various decolonial experiences" (TLOSTANOVA, 2012, p.64). In this way, the subject would be able to overcome the colonial marks of normative Western aesthetics, acquiring or creating their own aesthetic principles, emanating from their own local history.

Based on decolonial thinking centered on other ways of understanding the world, we may be able to rethink educational processes and, in particular, teaching processes focused on art/education. These educational processes should be thought of as collective strategies for generating meaning in shared life experiences, a form of cultural and social intertwining.

3 DECOLONIAL OPTION IN ART/EDUCATION

> Art in education opposes the supposed educational truths and even more suspect certainties of the school.
>
> *Ana Mae Barbosa*

Art in school education is pointed out in various studies as a victim of curricular planning and its institutional support instruments and, for this reason, faces problems of different kinds in terms of its affirmation in the regular education system. This situation presents characteristics that must be elucidated before thinking about decolonial paths and options for this area of knowledge in the school space. For this debate, we consider, as stated by VICTORIO FILHO (2011, p.204), that the field of art in school education has a "double force":

> The first is its meek but effective force in **ratifying** truths and values that are enunciated and quite recurrent in the pedagogical practices of other curricular areas, in other words, values that are still dominant in the Brazilian social fabric, including moralism, sexist hygienism, heteronormativism, cultural segregation, etc. that contaminate epistemological ordering and creation and other investments in the institution of knowledge (VICTORIO FILHO, 2011, p.204).

In a divergent sense, the second force would be "the contribution that experience, treatment and aesthetic production makes to the formation of subjects" (VICTORIO FILHO, 2011, p.204). In this case, we are considering the political and emancipatory power of the formation of the subject as a producer of meanings, in their ability to generate discourses from aesthetic production. This makes the aesthetic experience fundamental from an educational point of view, as an instrument for empowering the subject, diverging from the objective of training aimed exclusively at creating labor for the productive system. On this point, Oliveira (2001) states that "as the school generally sees itself as a preparatory stage [...] the student is only a becoming, that is, a subject without a present who lives the prospect of a promised future" (2001, p. 225), and this may be another reason why it seems unnecessary to give students a voice, because whatever present information they bring us, nothing can be added in terms of thinking about a curriculum that prepares futures.

In this way, the project of modernity, based on the affirmative belief in technology and the insertion of the subject into the system of production of goods, has conformed the aesthetic and sensitive knowledge of the human being to its principles of scientific accuracy and neutrality. This situation relegates aesthetic experiences and sensitive knowledge to the background, and they are thus considered minor experiences rather than valid knowledge. Insofar as school education continues to be based on modern values and subjugated by the dictates of the market and emphasizing utilitarian training, art/education has been assigned a lower position in the hierarchy that distinguishes and classifies school subjects. This gives rise to a question I've heard many times in everyday school life: what is art in education for anyway?

As a result of this utilitarian culture, it is common for parents, students and teachers to question the legitimacy of art teaching. In this case, the reference point for the validity of the subject is whether or not it fails the student, whether or not it is part of the knowledge required to pass an official assessment, etc. In any case, art in education seems to run counter to what our society validates as knowledge necessary for the formation of the individual. Even if we admit that disregarding the cognitive element of this area of knowledge, as well as its usefulness in different professions linked to the cultural industry, is a mistake, it is difficult to break the legacy that art carries as an extracurricular activity or as entertainment devoid of functional meaning in the educational system. Ratifying the position of art/education as being in opposition to the techno-efficient school narrative, based on modern-coloniality, Menezes (2009) states that:

> Against the remnants of scientism, solidified since the 19th century, which has legitimized valid knowledge for human beings, it is necessary to assume the nature of aesthetic and sensitive knowledge that should not, and cannot, be justified through a formal logical discourse. Subjecting art to the scientific order would be tantamount to transforming it into a civilizing and disciplining apparatus for students - good students: socially integrated, globalized, without prejudice, etc. - denying them what is most essential and critical in their practice: **the perversion of order** (MENEZES, 2009, p. 57).

We can see in the author's idea of the "perversion of order" an aspect that completely diverges from the worldview that has been sustained in the school system and in modernity through the belief in the power of reason over emotion, the power of order over disorder and the power of science over imagination. In order to circumvent the hegemonic perspective, some art teachers resort to certain tactics in their daily lives that I recognize in this research as potentially decolonial attitudes. This is what I identify in the report collected through an interview with teacher Helio, who, referring to one of his tactics in school:

> It was noisy, my class was noisy, of course it was noisy! It really annoyed the management and other teachers. So I started using the tools I had. I said: man, I'm going to stop teaching in the classroom. I started working with the students like this, creating situations by area of interest to them and allowing

> them to organize themselves into groups and use other spaces in the school. [...] Then a colleague of mine said to me, "You're being called that teacher who doesn't teach". One day, in one of those school corridor conversations, I heard from a friend that two first-grade teachers were talking about that teacher who doesn't teach and only hangs around the playground: that teacher was me. [...] I didn't plan a lesson for everyone, but I did plan lessons for certain groups and obviously that divided attention. This could happen in the school as a whole. In my time in the classroom, I deconstructed the idea of classes, right? (HELIO, H. Interview given to Andre Dias Pires. Duque de Caxias, June 10, 2014).

Along the same lines of reorganizing school time and space, we have the account of Lara, also an art teacher in the Duque de Caxias municipal school system:

> One thing I did was to start treating the school space, the common school space (corridor, cafeteria, stairwell) as public space. And then I started taking the class out of the classroom to have lessons in the corridors. [...] I started subverting and having fun, despite the censorious looks at my attitude. My yardstick now is: if I'm having fun, the class is cool. I realized that this strange place started to become much more attractive to the students. (IARA, I. Interview granted to Andre Dias Pires. Duque de Caxias, June 10, 2014).

These "perversions of order" are practiced by teachers who, in the anonymity of everyday life, invent survival tactics inspired by "micro resistances that found micro freedoms" (JOSGRILBERG, 2005, p.75). These tactics reveal the contradictions and doubt the pre-established and thus manage to shift the boundaries of the modern-colonial system's domination in the school context. Often, in these cases, the curriculum structure does not follow a predetermined sequence. Its movement is that of the emergent necessity of unforeseen events in the classroom and is translated into the curriculum by the commitment to the unstructured. In the words of teacher lara,

> There were times when I proposed one thing and the class came up with another. Was I going to say no? And there were times when I was enchanted by something in the world and wanted to bring it here. I'm not going to bring it because I've planned something else? No! [...] There was a time, as soon as I started, when I used to plan things very carefully. This time for this, this time for that. Today, class time is always being negotiated. More and more, I've been coming up with simpler proposals, so that I have time. Time for chance, time for the unexpected. Sometimes there's no time, sometimes there's plenty of time, and that extra time is for us to be able to talk, for me to go to the back of the room and ask to learn the passinho (which I haven't learned yet), or to listen to what they're listening to, and they laugh at me because I didn't know it, or they laugh with shame because it's forbidden funk, and then they're surprised because I already knew some of the songs.

Through these examples we can see that the challenge towards a different pedagogy in art/education does not lie in disciplining theoretical-practical knowledge, ordering it into a didactic set of pertinent, valid or traditionally accepted themes in art. On the contrary, it may be legitimizing and accepting unpredictability itself as inherent to this type of knowledge, which differs completely from the modern structuring of school knowledge. In my opinion, such attitudes take art in school education in a potentially decolonial direction.

However, despite the fact that these everyday experiences and inventions continue to point to the subversion of curriculum notions (and thus enhance decolonial attitudes), this does not mean that art/education, unlike other areas of knowledge present in the school curriculum, previously eliminates or is immune to the influences of modern coloniality in the school context. Nascimento (2013), in an essay entitled "Colonialities in the relationship between education and visualities" asks an essential question: "are there colonialities or relationships of knowledge and power in the field of art/education?" (NASCIMENTO, 2013, p.7). According to the author, "This question can send shivers down the spine, because there is a romantic discursive strand that conceives of this field (art/education) as an idealized space, full of expressiveness, goodness and candor, without any kind of oppression or repression" (NASCIMENTO, 2013, p.7). This perspective referred to by the author remains in force in art/education in many discourses and practices, but contrary to it, in the sense of a critical and decolonial approach, it is essential that we work from the clear notion that the search for knowledge and the study of art, the aesthetic and the cultural are not historically and politically neutral practices, but deeply imbricated and committed to the colonial and imperial trajectories of the past and present.

It's worth remembering that the field of art and its respective constructions (art theory, art history, art philosophy, aesthetic appreciation, etc.), as well as the concept of art itself, are Western inventions of modernity and therefore share the aforementioned relations of coloniality of power and knowledge. An example of this is the construction of the concept of "aesthetics" linked to the concept of "beauty". In the West, the Greek concept of aisthesis, which refers to feeling, the five senses and affection, the emotions, was converted into aesthetics in the 17th century, becoming a philosophical doctrine to regulate taste. In this way, aesthetics came to designate a theory whose practice would be art. From then on, the European philosophical-aesthetic discourse built its own past on Greco-Roman art and managed to establish it as criteria and categories for feeling, valuing and theorizing. When aisthesis is related to the idea of beauty (endorsed by the criteria of the European bourgeoisie and intended as universal truth), it rules out any possibility that a different aesthetic experience could occur at a time before or in a space outside of modernity-coloniality.

It can be said, then, that these concepts remain naturalized and unchallenged in art/education as a whole, persisting in the understanding of art as universal knowledge, with essentialist, timeless characteristics that can be synthesized and organized in a curriculum based on a historicist approach (based on the history of Euro-American art), founded on notions of taste and beauty originating from the European bourgeoisie. This pedagogical approach to art/education subordinates all the so-called "minor arts" in its axes, thus not allowing for understanding and immersion in other cultural codes and other aesthetic experiences.

Therefore, one of the crucial aspects of moving towards a decolonial option in art/education is recognizing and being open to other meanings, other aesthetics that disobey and challenge the cognitive and aesthetic codes of modernity. In this debate, we can establish links between issues raised by decolonial authors and other authors interested in emancipatory propositions in the context of art/education with educational practices already underway through local mini-rationalities adopted by teachers that can be identified in attitudes of defiance (not negation) in relation to the modern-colonial artistic canon, the valorization of local knowledge regarding cultural and artistic forms and other aesthetic expressions, and the perception of critical attitudes towards colonial difference, which includes full recognition of the epistemic asymmetries and geo-aesthetic hierarchies operated by coloniality. Although many educational practices prefer the apparent security of compulsory, prescriptive curricula, which reduce knowledge to a series of fragmented contents disconnected from reality, and thus perpetuate the relations of coloniality in force, it was possible to observe in the monitoring carried out at the Mauro de Castro Municipal School and in the interviews with art teachers from Duque de Caxias indications of educational experiences in development in the area of art/education, full of decolonial potential.

3.1 Approach to difference and identity constructions

Black people aren't. Neither is the white man.

Frantz Fanon

Establishing a reflection on decolonial alternatives for art/education in peripheral school spaces in the face of a predominantly monocultural, racist, classist and sexist educational system involves thinking about the relationship between hegemony and subalternity in classroom spaces as a problem that develops in constant cultural and political struggles. In this sense, it is important to discuss how concepts linked to the notion of difference and identity, such as "cultural diversity", "multiculturalism" and "interculturalism", which today constitute guiding principles for art/education, have been interpreted.[9]have been interpreted. These concepts, used as synonyms in various contexts (RODRIGUES, 2013, p.7), bring with them a polysemy through which the meanings of "difference" are often interpreted as a benign variation (diversity) and as a simple observation, based on a "politically correct" position that reproduces and maintains white Western hegemony under well-intentioned pluralist disguises (JAGODZINSKI, 2008 p.662). The very conceptualization of decolonial art/education already presupposes the recognition of a key problem about the role of Others, and who holds the power to produce these Others in Western modernity, especially in the context of various imperialisms and colonialisms.

Historically, studies on cultural plurality in education have been generated by ethnic/racial social movements (CANDAU; RUSSO, 2010) through demands for bilingual education for indigenous peoples in Latin America, through concerns and discussions to respond to the cultural diversities produced by mass access to schooling and took shape in the United States in the 1960s with multiculturalism as part of a movement in search of more equal opportunities in the social, political and, above all, educational spheres for marginalized groups.

In Brazilian art/education, since the 1980s, discussions about culture, cultural diversity and interculturality have become the principles of a teaching perspective that has been widely disseminated in research and by the National Curriculum Parameters (PCNs). Ana Mae Barbosa played an important role in this process in which "the commitment to cultural diversity is emphasized by art education" (2002, p.19). In the same vein, interculturality is one of the principles that has often been discussed when it comes to art education. Ivone Mendes Richter (2003) devotes special attention to the issue of multicultural education and interculturalism in art/education. According to the author, "in a world increasingly in conflict, multicultural education seeks to preserve culture and harmony through the development of intercultural skills". According to Richter (2003b, p.13-19):

> Multicultural education [...] involves developing competencies across many cultural systems. It recognizes similarities between ethnic groups or invests in highlighting differences, promoting the cultural crossing of boundaries between cultures, whatever they may be. [...] multicultural and intercultural education should familiarize students with the achievements of non-dominant cultures, so that they come into contact with other worlds, opening up to the

[9] Art/education has been influenced by a perspective that sees art no longer as standardized knowledge, nor as inner expression or language, but as a cultural fact. Hence the emphasis given by various authors, as well as by official curricular programs, to the treatment of issues related to plurality and cultural differences which, in this way, can be considered guiding principles of art/education in contemporary times.

> cultural richness of humanity (RICHTER, 2003b, p. 13-19).

In this way, the position adopted by the author accommodates a trend in art/education in which differences are being treated in terms of diversity and dialogue between reified cultures, rather than as a space for cultural and political struggles. There is a fear of emphasizing differences rather than similarities and thereby weakening social consensus. This tendency is demonstrated in art teacher Emerson's statement about tackling racism, homophobia and gender issues in elementary school:

> In elementary school, I find it difficult to introduce this type of question. There's a certain immaturity on their *(the students')* part when it comes to dealing with this kind of question. So, suddenly, you're going to point out something like this, with the best of intentions, and you end up creating more problems and not being able to find a solution. I think this is very delicate, you know? I see a lot of people working on racial issues specifically. I have some difficulty with these things. I look, I observe, I think it's nice and everything, but sometimes I think that, instead of contributing to greater integration, greater awareness of black people, respect, ethnic diversity and so on, we end up creating prejudice where it didn't exist. I followed the work of a teacher whose motto was the racial issue. She had one or two black pupils in her class. The children began to hate this business of talking about black people. Because they were there in the middle of it and it was quiet, nobody was talking about it.

Jan Jagodzinski (2005) criticizes the conservative approach to art education, in which difference is inserted in a policed, non-threatening way, without questioning the Western hegemony of art history, but only as an adjunct to the traditional curricular structure. In dealing with difference, this approach situates the "arts *per se*" using the "typical Eurocentric divisions, i.e. Islamic art history, oriental art history, 20th century contemporary art history" (JAGODZINSKI, 2005, p. 681). According to the author:

> In order to include their 'art' within existing classrooms, certain identifiable marks of stereotypical difference, racial idioms and semiotic systems of representation are created, which presuppose and affirm regulatory typifications and cultural stereotypes, making native cultures and non-white and non-Western peoples identifiable and usable in classrooms (JAGODZINSKI, p.665).

Diverging from these positions, we have the testimony of art teacher Mariane on the approach and problematization of differences in the arts curriculum in elementary school:

> It's important to say things to them. Sometimes a student brings up something very important, a suddenly prejudiced remark, and you pretend you don't hear it because you're doing your pretty art activity to make it look nice. But no, that's the subject of the lesson! Let's stop, let's talk and discuss it.

In a passage that took place during the monitoring carried out for this research at the Mauro de Castro Municipal School, we observed an intervention by teacher Mariane with the students when she showed an image that referred to candomble to the class and some students reacted by saying: "cruz credo!", "e macumba!". The teacher intervened:

> People, we are in a city with a very strong blackness! Why is it that everything related to black people, be it hair, words, dance or religion, is seen as a bad thing? And why do we blacks and mestiços continue to inferiorize it?

Despite the teacher's position, which encourages students to question difference and identity, serving as an example for a different pedagogy in art/education, both multiculturalism and interculturalism continue to be interpreted in curriculum documents and in the practices of many teachers through the simple and economical principle of adhering to certain "different" cultural and identity forms without, however, delving into the question of differences as deriving from power relationships and as perpetuating social inequalities. In the art/education curriculum, this means adding "other cultures" - marked by signifiers such as craft, folklore, mass, and primitive - to the cultural pattern of the grand narrative of art history. In this case, addressing cultural diversity is, at best, a way of getting to know and reaffirming the pattern and development of hegemonic Western, white and heterosexual culture.

This accommodation of cultural diversity is described by Jagodzinski (2008, p.667) in such a way that the classification of cultures as "the Other" is organized on the basis of the absence of "white" in this representation. For the author, these curricula are racist even if, at the same time, they appear to be anti-racist. Silva (2014) addresses the issue as follows:

> In a white supremacist society, for example, "being white" is not considered an ethnic or racial identity. In a world governed by US cultural hegemony, "ethnic" is the music or food of other countries. It is homosexual sexuality that is "sexualized", not heterosexual sexuality. The homogenizing force of normal identity is directly proportional to its invisibility (SILVA, 2014, p. 83).

In this case, the notion of "difference" is interpreted as a variation and confused with the idea of benign, assimilationist diversity rather than raising a more fundamental question concerning difference in terms of power relationships. Therefore, an art/education in which multiculturalism is based on forms of understanding and communication produces new dichotomies such as "hegemonic but benevolent identity" and subaltern but "respected identity" (SILVA, 2014, p. 98) and, furthermore, prevents us from seeing differences and processes of identification as social constructions.

The invention of the Other, based on the affirmation of white racial superiority, lies at the base of the world-system in modern coloniality (WALLERSTEIN apud CASTRO-GOMEZ and GROSFOGUEL, 2008, p.9). The Other, in this case, is "the other gender, the other and the different color, the other and the other sexuality, the other and the different body" (SILVA, 2014, p.97). For Quijano (2000), the process of social classification based on the idea of race, gender and work were the three main lines that allowed the formation and perpetuation of modern/coloniality. For the author, coloniality "is based on the imposition of a racial/ethnic classification of the world's population as the cornerstone of the so-called pattern of power and operates on each of the material and subjective planes, ambits and dimensions of everyday social existence and the social scale" (QUIJANO, 2000, p.342).[10]. This constitutes what Mignolo (2003) called colonial difference, the organizing principle that structures the hierarchy of identities and differences, whose fundamental mark is the identification of peoples according to their faults or excesses, produced and reproduced by the coloniality of power, knowledge and being.

The notion of colonial difference developed by Mignolo (2002, 2003) places great importance on the locus of enunciation of this difference. And here we have the epistemic and epistemological dimension, linked to modern-colonial Eurocentrism. In other words, the coloniality of knowledge. Eurocentrism is a fundamental logic for the reproduction of the coloniality of knowledge, as Quijano explains:

> The intellectual elaboration of the process of modernity has produced a perspective of knowledge and a way of producing knowledge that demonstrate the character of the global pattern of power: colonial/modern, capitalist and Eurocentric. This perspective and concrete way of producing knowledge is recognized as Eurocentrism. Eurocentrism is, here, the name of a perspective of knowledge whose systematic elaboration began in Western Europe before the middle of the 17th century, although some of its roots are undoubtedly older, or even ancient, and which, in the following centuries, became globally hegemonic, following in the footsteps of the dominance of bourgeois Europe (QUIJANO, 2005, p. 9).

In this way, European bourgeois culture historically established itself as hegemonic and took its production as universal and absolute truth. It should be understood that Eurocentrism is not only considered here as a cognitive, epistemological perspective of Europeans or, exclusively, of those who have dominated and dominate the world, but also of those who have been dominated by Eurocentric hegemony (QUIJANO, 2009).

Transposed to the context of art, this hegemonic position is maintained due to the way it has been defined and institutionalized in the West by the grand narrative of art history. According to Jagodzinski (2005, p. 665), firstly, art history has always maintained a national character, in other words, the constitution of nationality has always been linked to cultural forms of production. Secondly, modern is an individualistic form of expression, different from the artistic forms of non-Western

[10] Our translation.

cultures that do not bear the signature of the artist, but of the "whole tribe", which lacks historical development. Thirdly, authenticity and the guarantee of economic value are attributes attached to the artist's signature. In this way, the heroic history of male art repeats the binary logic of modern-coloniality. For multiculturalist art/education, there is no escape if it remains tied to art that is already predetermined by Enlightenment ideas of individuality, the avant-garde, progress, the value and originality of art, the talent of the artist and the economic value of the work.

Another perspective for this reflection is pointed out by the "decolonial option" defended by the modernity-coloniality group through a theoretical and practical, political and epistemological resistance movement that offers a different perspective for understanding and acting in the world, marked by the permanence of coloniality, at the different levels of personal and collective life. In the face of subalternized cultures, the decolonial option acts by expanding epistemological boundaries, with an emphasis on singular experiences, the translation and articulation of differences around heterogeneous and multifaceted collectivities, the recognition of subjects and their voices. Decoloniality makes room for continuous learning from the other, maintaining a destabilizing and decisive stance in re-reading the discursive constructs that have obstinately shaped Western thought, promoting colonial difference, which renders the subject subaltern and silenced.

Being aware of the implications of the universalist discourse of modern coloniality, as well as the appropriations of the Other (under the guise of benevolence and support), is of the utmost importance in the pedagogical and curricular context. However, this finding still doesn't answer the problem: what other directions can be taken? How can we think about identity, difference, diversity and cultural plurality in the context of school education? What can the decolonial option indicate in this regard?

For Catherine Walsh (2007), the answers point to an understanding of how the geopolitics of knowledge maintains a hierarchical system of racialization, the impact of which extends to the fields of identity. Thus, the author develops her argument by considering the coloniality of power, knowledge and being in the field of education, which continue to contribute to the colonization of minds through the notion that science and epistemology are objective and neutral, and that certain people are better able to think than others. Walsh then calls for the implementation of a pedagogy and educational practices that are not only critical, but decolonial. To this end, the author presents critical interculturality as a decolonial epistemic political project:

> Critical interculturality [...] is a construction by and from people who have

> suffered a historical experience of submission and subalternization. It is a proposal and a political project that could also expand to include an alliance with people who also seek to build alternatives to neoliberal globalization and Western rationality, and who struggle both for social transformation and for the creation of very different conditions of power, knowledge and being. Thought of in this way, critical interculturality is not an ethnic process or project, nor is it a project of difference in itself. [It is a project of existence, of life (WALSH, 2007, p. 8).

Walsh approaches the critical intercultural project with reference to Ecuador's Afro and Indigenous social movements, whose demand is to establish a position as a political strategy to avoid being totally consumed by the hegemonic universalization of modernity-coloniality. According to the author, this strategic intention differs from the intention to standardize or essentialize based on the idea of a stable and unified ethnic experience. It is in this sense that interculturality is not just understood as a new concept or term to refer to simple contact between the West and other civilizations, but as something inserted into a conceptual configuration that proposes an epistemic turn capable of producing new knowledge and another symbolic understanding of the world.

In this discussion, we extend an invitation to dialogue with a variety of intellectual critiques on the power and epistemology of colonialism and its legacies in the present. In this sense, we bring in the contribution of Bhabha (2003) who establishes an important distinction between cultural diversity - defined as a category - and cultural difference - defined as a process:

> If cultural diversity is a category of comparative ethics, aesthetics or ethnology, cultural difference is a process of signification through which statements about or in a culture differentiate, discriminate and authorize the production of fields of force, reference, applicability and capacity (BHABHA, 2003, p.34).

In this way, the author sees diversity as culture made into a thing, as an object of knowledge, from a perspective that sidelines questions of power. Whereas difference would be the process of enunciation of culture, the process of cultural construction, which is recognized as a space of dispute over power. By establishing his interest in the concept of cultural difference, rather than diversity, Bhabha (2003) discusses the prospect of placing the concept of multiculturalism in terms of hybridity, in which difference should be emphasized (negotiated) by incorporating other influences. According to the author, hybridity is a threat to cultural and colonial authority, subverting the dominant authority's concept of origin or pure identity through the ambivalence created by negation, variation, repetition and displacement. It is also a threat because it is unpredictable. These features of hybridity make it transgress the entire project of the dominant discourse and demand recognition of difference, questioning and shifting "the value of the symbol to the sign" of the authoritarian discourse (BHABHA, 2003, p.113). In the search for a non-racist culture, the assertion has been that the

> Identity is a matter of political rather than ontological contingency, a recognition that subjects are found "in the middle of" domains or liminal spaces of difference such as race, class and gender, in the interstices where these domains intersect. (JAGODZINKI, 2014, p. 672)

Stuart Hall (2013) puts it this way:

> The experience of diaspora, as I understand it in this context, is defined not by essence or purity, but by the recognition of a necessary heterogeneity and diversity: by the conception of "identity" that lives with and through difference, and not in spite of it: by hybridity. Diasporic identities are those that are constantly, once again, producing and reproducing themselves through transformation and difference (HALL, 2013, p. 235).

From what has been discussed, the most effective attitude against racism would be to be consciously always transforming oneself through the incorporation of difference. However, not everyone has the necessary conditions to engage in constant self-relativism. As Robert Stam and Ella Shohat (2006, apud MARTINS e SERVIO 2013, p.5) tell us, in fact, many cannot afford to relativize themselves in this "postmodernist" way:

> [...] much of postmodern theory is a sophisticated example of what Abdel Malek calls the 'hegemony of privileged minorities': the denial of the reality of marginalization is a luxury that only non-marginalized individuals can afford. The center proclaims the end of its privileges precisely when the periphery begins to demand them. All these distortions reflect a privilege available only to those who already have power, because the proclamation of the end of the margins does not extinguish the mechanisms that actually deprive people of their culture and nations of their power (STAM and SHOHAT 2006, apud MARTINS and SERVIO 2013 p. 5).

This perspective reminds us that those in an unequal position of symbolic power are forced to engage in a struggle for a positive representation rather than a stigmatized one, or even against the complete absence of representation. For these many, practices of signification such as identity politics are not something that can be given up in the name of total relativism. For these groups, the idealism involved in creating imagined communities (HALL 2011) is something they need to strengthen themselves. That's why they fight for a "strategic essentialism" (SPIVAK, 2010) that serves the emancipatory interests of those kept in conditions of subalternity.

In this sense, Jagodzinski (2008, p. 679) concludes that "both hybridism and essentialism present their own set of problems". Finally, he argues that alternative political strategies to the hegemonic narrative, "whether strategic essentialism or hybridity, cannot be promoted generically, but must always be placed in socio-historical terms and conditions" (JAGODZINSKI, 2008, p.679). Thus, we conclude by agreeing with Hall (2013, p.87) when he states that:

> What can no longer be sustained, in the face of the "multicultural" question, is the binary contrast between the particularism of "their" demand for recognition of difference versus the universalism of our civic rationality (HALL, 2013, p.87).

And so prejudice and misperceptions cannot be corrected simply by providing information about the other. Critical and culturally diverse pedagogical approaches depend on the values and attitudes of the actors involved. In this sense, decolonizing alternatives to modern-colonial oppression depend on the development of radically local and contextual social practices. According to Oliveira (2012, p.19), it is necessary not to lose sight of the fact that horizontal social and educational practices preclude the proposition of recipes for procedures and actions, and that it is necessary to consider the specificity of the different educational "time-spaces". This means that the development of alternative educational practices "must be contextually local in order to be legitimate" (OLIVEIRA, 2012, p.19).

3.2 Challenging the modern artistic canon

> In the same way, it is no longer Art (with a capital A) that should count as the substance here; it is no longer the aesthetic as an end, but above all as a means. This also leads to an increasingly necessary yet still incipient and hesitant renunciation of the very "status" of art, i.e. a detachment from and unconditional surrender to life.
>
> Ricardo Rosas

The search for knowledge and the study of art, aesthetics and culture do not correspond to historically and politically neutral practices, but are deeply intertwined and committed to the colonial and imperial trajectories of the past and present. Therefore, it follows that thinking about decolonial art/education in the school context implies a critical understanding of history, a repositioning of educational practices and, fundamentally, a decentering from the modern-colonial epistemic perspective in favor of other perspectives.

However, in proposing a disconnection from the modern-colonial lens in the context of school art/education, we are not advocating a search for a pure or essentialist identity with regard to aesthetic experiences and artistic productions that are considered to be proper or local. A decolonial educator would be self-conscious about the multiple uses, meanings and cultural hybrids related to the diverse ways of being, living, thinking, feeling and expressing oneself, as well as the processes of historical construction of the modern-colonial model, far removed from any form of simplification or generalization.

According to the above, knowledge of art, aesthetics and culture must be considered as a historical product, geopolitically delineated, linked to power interests that define, shape and establish it. Thus, we start from the understanding that its character is not absolute, universal or apolitical; on the contrary, it is a construction that obeys power relations that situate it historically, giving it a specific political place in the world. It is therefore necessary to concretely materialize this critical understanding through specific educational proposals that establish ways of acting on the modern-colonial epistemic perspective in order to problematize and reverse it.

With regard to this debate in the context of art/education, we must initially "recognize that art itself is a Western concept", "an object of the philosophical discourse of the Enlightenment" (JAGODZINSKI, 2008, p. 671) and, for this very reason, it needs to be relativized and understood also as a cultural construction of a specific historical context. Disregarding this Western and Enlightenment origin of the idea of art often implies imposing these criteria on the manifestations of other cultures. Jagodzinski (2008, p.665) tells us, for example, that criteria such as individuality and authenticity mean little to many "traditional" cultures. Thus, once the ideological boundaries of art are perceived and the limitations to which they condition the work of teachers, he assures us:

> An art education whose foundations remain entrenched in the notion of discipline, the Western canon of art, the art studio and the formalist principles of criticism, i.e. modernism, has very little hope of accomplishing anything more than the reincorporation of "neo-racist" strategies of confinement (JAGODZINSKI, 2008, p. 683).

Still on the subject of the work of art teachers in the school context, the author acknowledges that "it seems highly unlikely that art teachers will abandon the fine arts tradition, i.e. the Western canon of great works of art, and rewrite their programs with a different focus" (JAGODZINSKI, 2008, p.684). However, the author stresses that he is not advocating such an abandonment, but rather an attitude of "disaffiliation" from the modern artistic canon, leading to a re-evaluation of Euro-American narcissism. I recognize in this disaffiliatory attitude proposed by him a decolonial option already adopted in art/education through the practices developed by some teachers. We can see that this process can begin with the recognition of the distance between canonical and school art in relation to the aesthetic experiences of the students, as demonstrated by teacher Emerson, according to whom "this thing of teaching artistic movements, this historicized art, from the European point of view, etc. really communicates very little with the students". Still exemplifying this point, teacher Iara says in her statement:

> I have no problem with this issue of Eurocentrism. I have a problem if that's all there is to it. That's all there is to it. You can also show an Art History class, spit chalk on the board, only if you're too lazy. It doesn't affect the student, they may even find it strange, but it's too strange, they don't get into it. (IARA, I. Interview granted to Andre Dias Pires. Duque de Caxias, June 10, 2014).

Following this stance, the teacher problematizes the exclusivity of the "universality" of art and artistic productions, when they are profiled and valued only in terms of their contributions to rhetoric and the modern normative universe of art history. In this way, the small spaces granted to the multiple aesthetic experiences of each student, for example, are privileged to the detriment of the great hegemonic accounts of canonical art history. In this way, it is possible to establish a parallel with the problematization of the modern-colonial ideals embedded in the canon of Western art, based on a linear history, constructed by a succession of events, epochs and styles that, consecutively, provide a subalternizing apartment, in relation to other aesthetic experiences and cultures.

These concepts developed in modern-coloniality have been naturalized in art/education, persisting in an understanding of art as universal knowledge, with essentialist, timeless characteristics, which can be synthesized and organized in a curriculum based on a historicist approach (based on the history of Euro-American art), the identification of formal relationships and stylistic aspects and based on some technical learning.

This approach subordinates all the so-called "minor cultures" in its support, thus not allowing them to understand and immerse themselves in other cultural codes and other aesthetic experiences. According to Aguirre (2009, p. 159), in this way, students' contact with the so-called "cultured arts" is restricted to school practices, associated with a means of achieving social recognition. Such relationships trigger an "immediate refraction", because the "connection between curricular materials and young people's aesthetic repertoires is completely lacking or nil". This gap between the school curriculum and the repertoire of the young student would prevent the transformation of "high culture products and the visual arts" into an instrument of relevance to the "vital experience of these young people", becoming part of the collection of "school knowledge alien to the world and completely inoperative as shapers of their identity" (AGUIRRE, 2009, p.160). According to Aguirre (2009, p.7), art must be understood as a "lived experience". To do this, it is necessary to "neutralize its elitist character", stripping art of its "transcendental dimension" attributed by the modern tradition. It is necessary to understand art as part of our lives, as an object, a production, a historical and cultural manifestation, "accepting that meanings can change with changing practices and realities that condition our experiences" (AGUIRRE, 2009, p.7). In establishing his concept of art and defining the scope of his educational work, the author states that:

> It's not a question of imposing supposedly refined art forms on others that we believe are not. On the contrary, it's about making the enrichment of the sensitive capacity to live aesthetically (and ethically) the centerpiece of educational action [...] conceiving art as an experience and the work as an open account offers a privileged starting point for improving students' motivation for art education, because it allows them to include, as an object of study, the artifacts of their own aesthetic culture, thus promoting greater integration between their vital experiences of art (AGUIRRE, 2009, p. 8).

This conception is in line with Professor Helio's account when he states that:

> The idea is not to aim for a set of contents that will make students more culturally "polished". On the contrary, the main objective is to make them discover their own creative and political potential. And to explode the "naturalization" of their existential condition! [...] We think of art as a detonating element that explodes patterns. (HELIO, H. Interview granted to Andre Dias Pires. Duque de Caxias, June 10, 2014).

This reading is in line with Jagodizinski (2008, p. 685) when he says that, in art/education, the established artistic canon should be read as a "disaffiliatory discourse", "integrating and deconstructing its binarisms". This means identifying the exclusions on which it was based, especially subaltern aesthetic productions, which have been discredited in order to perpetuate established aesthetic notions in which categories such as taste, for example, become a consequence of power relations that cross within and between cultural groups. We should point out that, for Jagodzinski (2008), the disaffiliatory attitude he suggests neither removes nor diminishes canonized art as an exceptional human achievement. Rather, defiance corresponds to an attitude of destabilization of Euro-American narcissism. In this way, teachers and students can begin to "de-canonize" the classics according to alternative perspectives. In the words of Professor Helio:

> No one will deny that expressionism is interesting, there is something cool about it. The point is that there's more to it than that, and expressionism isn't the only important thing in the world connected to art. Not art, not anything! Any subject we have to put into context, there's no way. (HELIO, H. Interview granted to Andre Dias Pires. Duque de Caxias, June 10, 2014).

This alternative, challenging perspective can be seen in the following passage during art teacher Mariane Travassos' lessons at the Mauro de Castro secondary school: the teacher showed the students in class 802 (eighth grade) images of human figures in classical Greek and Roman art, telling them that this type of representation of the human body "has become a standard and a model of beauty". At the same time, the teacher questioned the class: "But what is this model?", "Why does this model exist?". While the students were blurting out their comments, the teacher showed them a picture of a magazine with a model in a bikini. This image provoked more disquiet in the students, who made comments such as: "Wow, she's hot!" Teacher Mariane then asked: "Why is this woman hot? Come on guys, I want more, why do we say that this guy or this woman is a Greek god or a Greek goddess? Does that have a story? At one point, the teacher used her own "standard of beauty" as an example: "Is my hair hard? Is it ugly? Is it bad? Where do these expressions come from?

In this way, Mariane produced a discussion with her students based on an image of canonical art, not with the sole aim of transmitting knowledge of art history, teaching about its formal or stylistic characteristics, but to deconstruct the notions of beauty derived from the "universal laws" of aesthetics that fix, classify and stereotype, based on coloniality, what beauty is, what black people are, what indigenous people are, what the lower classes are. For Professor Mariane Travassos,

> The problem isn't choosing between one curriculum or another. In relation to art/education, it's about turning this history of art on its head, because it's the history of art of the hegemon, of Europe, which sees all other productions as folkloric, primitive, and that's still the case today, isn't it? (TRAVASSOS, M. Interview granted to Andre Dias Pires. Duque de Caxias, June 10, 2014).

By recognizing in their pedagogical practice the close relationship between the construction of knowledge and the exercise of power, it becomes clear that the apparent technical neutrality and objectivity adopted by a knowledge (through curricula, pedagogical models, didactics, etc.) are, in reality, constructed through power struggles at certain historical moments. In this sense, by calling for a defiance of the modern-colonial artistic canon, we are talking about a posture, a decolonial attitude that can be adopted by art teachers. It is a posture of disengagement and critical re-evaluation in relation to the tradition of universal art history, aesthetics and disciplinary theories of art, which acts by identifying the exclusions on which it is based.

3.3 Dialogue with local cultural and aesthetic productions

For Marin (2009), "the approach to the relationship between local knowledge and universal knowledge, imposed by the dominant culture, is the main reference for the theoretical proposition of the decolonization of knowledge" (MARIN, 2009, p.1).

Taking this statement as a basis, I believe that in order to follow a decolonial bias, art/education must take as a reference the approach of the relationships between aesthetic experiences, local cultural and artistic productions in the school context. This means countering the values of a European universalism with those of a local pluriversalism, remaining open to the intersection of multiple uses and meanings of the aesthetic and the artistic. These opposing impulses lead us to think of a decolonial option for art/education in which "the subject removes the colonizing cloaks of normative Western aesthetics and acquires or creates its own aesthetic principles, emanating from its own local history" (TLOSTANOVA, 2011, p.63).

In this sense, Dussel (2005) proposes a dialogue that points to a pluriversal (not universal) utopia, in which the margins dialogue with each other without the mediation of the center: a movement emanating from the periphery to the periphery. According to Dussel, this idea of a margin-margin approach must point to the reconstruction of our own cultural traditions, which must be studied consciously and in depth,

> [...] The affirmation of one's own values requires time, study, reflection, a return to the texts or symbols and myths that constitute one's own culture, before or at least at the same time as the mastery of the texts of hegemonic modern culture (DUSSEL, 2005, p. 22).

This is in line with the aims of decolonial pedagogy, which reflects on the relationship between local and global knowledge, leading us to think about the power relations between dominant and dominated cultures. However, we note that arguing in favour of "affirming one's own values" or "one's own culture" can lead to a binary fixation of essentialized identities, when, in contrast to this, the antagonism presupposed by the concept of colonial difference (MIGNOLO, 2003) does not arise from full and fixed identities, but from the impossibility of constituting other indenitarian representations, outside of the modern-colonial model. Therefore, by rejecting the colonial lens and proposing the affirmation of local experiences, we are not proposing a return to a pure, essentialist identity, nor to folk art, but rather the creation and valorization of different spaces of enunciation and empowerment of subalternized subjects and cultural groups. This attitude is in line with what art teacher Francine says when she talks about her educational practice:

> I can talk about Van Gogh, African art, I can talk about the artist on the corner, I can talk about television... My final intention is to make the guy appropriate any discourse. Make him own his speech in some way at a given moment. (FRANCINE, F. Interview granted to Andre Dias Pires. Duque de Caxias, June 10, 2014).

We can think of a decolonial pedagogical experience in art/education by drawing a parallel with what Madina Tlostanova (2012) calls the "decolonial anti-sublime" when thinking about art and aesthetic experiences from a decolonial approach, stating that it is,

> It tries to heal a colonized mind and soul, freeing the person from colonial inferiority complexes, and allowing them to feel that they too are a human being with dignity, that they too are beautiful and valuable as they are. The audience sought by decolonial art is internally plural and its collectivity is founded on difference, not equality (Tlostanova, 2012, p.64).

The focus of this problematization is on overcoming the need to elaborate Western or European thinking in order to be accepted as a human being (a condition that is not guaranteed), starting from a shift towards recognizing and opening up to other logics, other thoughts and other aesthetics, valuing the pluriversality of existing epistemes and types of knowledge that otherwise remain subalternized.

In schools, this movement can only be possible by opening up and getting closer to the circumstantial and contextual knowledge that circulates in the community where they live. This thought is in line with what Professor Helio says, referring to the context of art/education in peripheral schools:

> For me, it would basically be listening, bringing in the community. Because we don't know what the cultural, artistic and aesthetic manifestations of these people are. Nobody knows that there is cultural and artistic production in the Baixada Fluminense. [...]. In fact, this is the knowledge that we don't know what it is. Something we don't know. If we listen, we can try to exchange ideas and present what we know. (HELIO, H. Interview given to Andre Dias Pires. Duque de Caxias, June 10, 2014).

However, in general, schools continue to be based on the educational purpose of transmitting disciplinary knowledge that seeks, above all, to legitimize itself and the type of worldview it mediates. Above all, hegemonic views that exclude and leave on the margins many other existing perspectives and representations of indenity, in relation to local experiences and knowledge.

Teacher Lara's account of her experience at the school where she works goes some way towards identifying these difficulties:

> I feel this a lot at school: a huge fear of the community. How are you going to understand the community as part of the school if you are afraid of these people? [...] this fear has a perverse relationship with the popular space, a relationship of great prejudice.

Hence the importance of pointing out indications for the development of a different educational project, which treats students and the local community as bearers of diverse social memories, with the right to speak and represent themselves in the search for learning and self-affirmation. Professor Mariane questions the maintenance of current curricula that focus on the works and collections chosen by the official history of art as what is worth dealing with in the context of art/education in peripheral school spaces:

> How are you going to affirm, reinforce, certain concepts of art history, of the art world of the market, of galleries, of museums, when the understanding of artistic production in a given community doesn't necessarily correspond to what's in the museum? Suddenly, what is in the museum, what is in the traditional curriculum invalidates what is in the community in which you are working.

The teacher continues and deepens her questioning in relation to the inferiorization of students' aesthetic experiences and the processes of subjectivation linked to them, highlighting the disregard for these issues by many teachers:

> [...] so their (the students') choices, aesthetic preferences and culture are denied, because they are young, because it's a minor culture, as if they weren't citizens. And also because they're gay, because they're girls, because they're boys, because they're black and from the periphery... And with teenagers, this knowledge, these tastes, these aesthetics, which are a way of representing oneself, of showing oneself, of marking, of marking a way of thinking, are very evident in the classroom. But teachers in general don't see this as a legitimate aesthetic. It's more or less like this: "What I don't know, I'm afraid of, and I'll stigmatize it".

This panorama reveals the neglect with which peripheral cultures, their aesthetic productions, their visual and sound choices, their ways of seeing and expressing themselves are treated in schools. Despite their social strength and the cultural networks they make up, the aesthetic experiences that are the preferred target of students' interest and that represent the cultural places where young people find many of their references to build their subjectivity experiences are often not taken into account by teachers.

Escaping these curricular totalizations in art/education, there are other spaces being created, based on micro freedoms and legitimizing different subjects and knowledge (OLIVEIRA, 2012). In these spaces, the great universalizing narratives crumble and other possibilities are opened up for a much more detailed study that takes into account the circumstantial and contextual specificities related to local aesthetic experiences. This movement implies affirming the existence of aesthetic elements, both inside and outside the field of art, which call into question the very essence of the matrix of modernity - coloniality. This is what the educational experience narrated by art teacher Helio suggests:

> Funk is a problem at school. Because funk has this thing of being linked to marginality, treated as marginal, crime... There's also the eroticized funk thing, something that's not well regarded and so on. It's common to hear at school: "funk can't!". But how can I not talk about it? [...] AT, I give a lesson, "the history of funk by ear". I show the songs... I show James Brown, who is considered the father of funk. I ask: "Why is he the father of funk?" I wait for the kids to say something and then I say: "because he was the first black man to be accepted into American society". [...] Then I go and talk about the concept of periphery. I explain to them that the periphery is not a geographical

concept, but a socio-cultural and economic one. I show them a picture of Capao Redondo, I show them a picture of Rocinha, I explain where the name favela came from, canudos and so on... I talk about cultural differences, I show MC Creu, Mano Brown, gaiola das popozudas and I show the Antonias of Hip Hop. And then I explain how carioca funk came about, which is another kind of funk compared to American funk, but which has its value.... I play "I'm ugly, but I'm fashionable"[1311]. I go to Sao Paulo, I show the politicized periphery, hip-hop, I show the Racionais video, then I talk about graffiti and show the Gemeos, I talk about Break and show Nelson Triunfo... The kids instantly identify! [...] When I teach this funk class, the teacher who enters the room doesn't leave. He just stares... "I didn't know, I didn't know"... Al, he can even change his perspective on funk. And that's fundamental!

By means of this report, we don't mean that the students' life experiences and aesthetic preferences should be pedagogized, but that, from them, connections can be made with research issues such as cultural differences, subaltern aesthetics, classism, sexism and the affirmation of marginalized identity constructions, for example. Therefore, the identification that students feel with certain aesthetic expressions, such as funk, is not an aspect to be recriminated or repressed, but to be transformed into questions about the role they play in the construction of their subjectivities.

[11] I'm ugly, but I'm fashionable" (directed by Denise Garcia) is a documentary about funk carioca released in 2005 that highlights the presence and importance of women in this movement. The name of the film is attributed to a phrase by the singer Tati Quebra-Barraco who said: "When I started, people said: 'Oh, what about that girl who sings that song? But she's ugly! I said: 'I am, but I'm fashionable'."

Another way of incorporating decolonial elements into educational practices is to establish links with knowledge generated from community cultural and artistic practices, drawing on experiences where alternative ways of producing knowledge have been developed. These relationships can potentially foster, in a wider and interconnected context, links and networks around ideals, projects and experiences of social transformation with sufficient epistemic and political reach to question and counter the established hegemonic order.

An example of the possibility of dialogue between local cultural producers and the school took place at the Mauro de Castro Secondary School where, during the period of monitoring and data collection for this research (November 2014), an audiovisual workshop was held with students from the 7th year of elementary school with a well-known group of cultural supporters linked to audiovisual in Duque de Caxias: the Mate com Angu film club.

The workshop was created at the request of the art teacher and her students, who at the time wanted to study and work in art classes with the film "Lixo Extraordinario" by artist Vik Muniz, produced in the same community where the Mauro de Castro school is located, in the Jardim Gramacho district, very close to the former dump (now a controlled landfill), which received almost all the waste disposed of by the city of Rio de Janeiro and the surrounding area. Teacher Mariane assumed that the students were interested in the subject, since many of them, like their parents, are or have been waste pickers in the locality. The fact that some of the students already knew the documentary filmed between 2007 and 2009 didn't surprise her, but we discovered that, for the students, the film had another name: "the ramp film". "What about the ramp, teacher?" the students asked, referring to the ramp where the garbage trucks dumped the waste and materials disputed by the waste pickers. A striking scene from the documentary and probably from their own lives. One of the teacher's first moves was to ask the students if they personally knew some of the people who took part in the film. The answers were positive. Zumbi, a character in the documentary, worked near the school. Zumbi couldn't be found, but the search for him in the community led to contacts with recyclers, which represented a rich and unexpected exchange of knowledge, not only about the experience of the community's participation in the artist's film, but also about technical and economic aspects.

related to recycling. In addition, the recyclers donated a large quantity of granulated plastic material to the art project (very interesting plastically) and came to the school to take part in discussions about the film with the class and the art teacher. One of the issues discussed at the time was, for example, whether or not the work with art presented in the film had generated any social change in the community. After the debate, with the desire to understand how a film is produced, contact was made with Mate com Angu for an audio visual workshop at the school.

The workshop, held over two days at E.M. Mauro de Castro, was led by cultural producer Heraldo HB who, using audiovisual examples, taught about the main cinematographic shots, notions of editing and editing, but above all, the enormous power of telling one's own story. In this sense, Heraldo HB began his talk with the students while simultaneously holding a camera and continuously filming class 702. This was the beginning of the dialogue:

> Heraldo - Guys, I'm going to talk to you about something very serious. In the history of the world, there has been one thing, the greatest weapon ever invented by human beings: the camera and the great weapon! Today, images are everywhere. Everyone here is recorded, and filmed, filmed... It's no use! Images are everywhere: movies, telephones... Everywhere has a screen, so learning about audiovisuals gives you an idea of how you can use the screen to speak or present an idea you want to present.
>
> Heraldo - Engrapado, when I'm filming you, most of you are hiding. Why is that?

> Student - Because he thinks he's ugly.
>
> HB - Exactly! You're brought up to think you're ugly! From childhood you're brought up like this: you're ugly, you're disjointed, you're stupid... Everything bad... And on television you see a fantasy world that doesn't show the Brazilian people. [...] So what's changing in the world today is that we're able to tell our story. So what I do, the work of cinema, is a job of showing that we can show our reality.
>
> Student - Because we take it out of reality so you can put it into the business we're doing...
>
> Heraldo - I told you that the camera has power over us. And understanding the power of the camera is important for living in this world.

Through this workshop experience, it was possible to see that establishing dialogues with cultural movements and groups such as Mate com Angu is an important way of bringing together the knowledge produced at school with that which emerges from the communities in which they operate. It is a question of investing in micropolitical processes, based on the consideration that these contacts produce knowledge that mediates experiences and subjectivities that encourage subjects to seek their own ethical, political, social, creative, epistemic and existential agency. In this way, investing in dialogue with the cultural and artistic productions and aesthetic manifestations of the community constitutes fertile ground for the generation of unpredictable emergencies and emotional ruptures that can be converted into symbolic, aesthetic and political ruptures that lead to the recovery of sensitivities, postures, attitudes and other experiences through strategies of disengagement from coloniality in the fields of art and aesthetics. In this sense, these experiences potentially represent a significant decolonial option for art/education in peripheral school spaces, allowing us to think about new ways of approaching aesthetic productions and, with this, educational processes.

4 PERSPECTIVES TOWARDS ANOTHER WAY OF THINKING

I come to the end of this piece of writing sure that I have achieved my goal of contributing to the discussion on the development of reflections that allow us to outline conditions and possibilities in the direction of a decolonial option in the context of art/education in peripheral school spaces. Aware, however, that I have not reached the end of the possibilities for exploring the research, I would like to emphasize that the considerations I have tried to develop do not intend to cover a supposed totality of the issues in the direction of a decolonial pedagogy in art/education (which would be impossible), the intention of this research being to initiate a reflexive action around this theme.

It is only possible to start debating ideas about a different and decolonial pedagogy in peripheral school contexts, in the field of art/education, or any other field of knowledge, if we initially consider the close relationship of educational thought with the networks of power that have operated in modernity through coloniality, remaining aware that the school, as a modern institution par excellence, represents one of the main devices that materialize and perpetuate relations of coloniality. However, as we have tried to demonstrate through this research, we recognize in school education experiences, subjects and knowledge that represent signs and possibilities of other, decolonial pedagogies. Practices that are already underway, which permeate today's school scenarios and create spaces where the critical gaze and the decolonial attitude constitute an epistemic perspective that disobeys the modern parameters of control and organization of education. These decolonial attitudes develop when the subject becomes aware of their place in the colonial matrix of power. When this happens, they realize that they are hierarchized by a structure organized to produce differences. This structure is coloniality, in which universalism, sexism and racism are fundamental elements.

During this investigation, through the contact I had with other teachers in the interviews and during the day-to-day monitoring, I was able to see some indications of what a "decolonial educator" would be in the field of art/education. Although these characteristics cannot be pre-determined from an idealized, ready-made or stable profile, we can see some attitudes present in the practices of educators who are already making a difference, who have in common the questioning of the modern-colonial heritage in education. Among the attitudes that we believe are fundamental in the direction of decolonial pedagogies are: openness to other meanings - different from those of modern-coloniality - which is based on valuing particular and local histories; concern and reflexive action about difference, subalternity, new subjectivities, the "Other"; a deconstructive attitude towards knowledge and values that claim to be universal in modern-coloniality.

With regard to a pedagogical approach that problematizes differences and identity constructions in the context of art/education, we have noticed that, in the educational practices of some teachers, there is sometimes a dialectic between a tendency towards assimilative accommodation as opposed to confronting the daily practice of difference in the classroom. The multiplicity of interpretations and pedagogical situations in art/education has not contributed to the stabilization or condensation of a meaning for the treatment of issues linked to the treatment of difference, subalternity, the "Other" and new subjectivities in terms of opting for a provisional essentialism or in relation to an anti-essentialist hybridism. From what has been analyzed, there is no way to predetermine the most effective attitudes towards these issues in the educational context, whether it is to assume exclusively a position in favor of policies of affirmation of inferior identities in the face of the hegemonic narrative, or to refuse an essentialist classification in which the subaltern can appear as the constitution of yet another "other". However, I understand that, according to a decolonial pedagogical approach, it is not up to the teacher to avoid or ignore the focus on differences as a result of power relationships or to perceive students only as beings of cognition, but rather to perceive them as sociocultural beings, in constant transformation of their subjectivities and identifications. I conclude that these positions can only be taken in a contextual and particular way, within the pedagogical situation experienced. I then turn to the well-known concept of Santos (2003) when he says that "we have the right to be equal when our difference makes us inferior; and we have the right to be different when our equality makes us unequal". The main focus of the research was to discuss the openness that can lead to the development of potentially decolonial and emancipatory curricular practices in the context of art/education. In this sense, with

Certeau (1995, 2008), through his commitment to narrating "common practices", the "arts of doing" of practitioners, made it possible to talk about other pedagogies, investigating decolonial signs in the creations and arts of/in everyday school life.

These practices are exercised as forms of resistance, that is, as ways of circumventing established policies and practices, based on educational insurgencies that represent the construction of other political, cultural and epistemological conditions.

In this sense, we have seen both in the monitoring of daily school life carried out at the E.M. Mauro Castro and in the interviews with the art teachers. Mauro de Castro and in the interviews conducted with art teachers, the willingness of the research subjects to purposefully break away from the usual organization of school space-time, for example, in relation to the grouping of students, the teacher as the only source for broadening the horizon of knowledge and even in accepting the impossibility of predetermining the possible subjects for an art class, demonstrating a willingness to learn from what is emerging, from what is happening and not just from what is established and recognized in art/education. I identify decolonial potential here, because these attitudes mean revising the influence of modernity on the school, especially the one that establishes the priority function of teaching "the essentials" of certain subjects transformed into school materials. It is necessary to revise and question this tradition, when we know that the consideration of what is "essential" is also based on relationships of opportunity and power.

In the debate around possibilities for a decolonial pedagogy, we therefore problematize the imposition of predetermined formulas on educational procedures and support in art/education, valuing the consideration of the specificities of different learning spaces and times. In this sense, we can point to what is intended by identifying the attitude of disaffiliation from the modern artistic canon: discussing and stimulating openness to other meanings, capable of fragmenting the parameters imposed by modern thinking through the coloniality of power. This corresponds to an attitude of disengagement from the cultivation of a gnosiological and ontological slavery to the rhetoric of modernity. Therefore, if, on the one hand, modern educational thinking favors the teaching of objective disciplinary knowledge, without a subject, considered universal and validated as the only epistemic register from which human formation is possible, on the other hand, from the perspective of a decolonial pedagogy, it is fundamental to postulate the opening up to other possible routes of knowledge that include the subject as the main protagonist and allow the creation of others, different to those hegemonically instituted as valid and legitimate.

This type of disaffiliatory attitude can be seen in the analysis of the data from this research, when teachers give examples of positions that consciously problematize the Eurocentrism of artistic content, the recognition of the distance between school art and the aesthetic experiences of students, when they try, through their interventions, to interpret and respond to what affects the construction of the subjectivities of those who go to school. As has been shown, this requires the appropriation of other knowledges and other ways of exploring and interpreting reality, since decoloniality implies acting on different dimensions of knowledge and being (i.e. subjectivity) by putting the ethics and politics of knowledge "upside down". It is therefore plausible to note that, on the road to a decolonial pedagogy in art/education, it is essential not only to focus on the need for a critical analysis of the forms of representation that reproduce and legitimize the colonial matrix, but also to broaden the process in order to use and value aesthetic experiences, based on the diversity of uses, knowledge and possible forms of aesthetic expression generated by a given community.

In this sense, during this research we had examples of spaces created by teachers in their educational practices for the discussion of youth aesthetics and cultural manifestations of the local community. These spaces represent openings towards a decolonial pedagogy when networks are established between school art/education and the artistic manifestations and cultural supports that emerge from local communities. Even though we know that the link between school culture and the culture that emerges from the communities is not frequent in schools due to many limitations that cannot be discussed here, I believe that the opportunity to establish partnerships, such as the one between the Caxiense group Mate com Angu and the art classes at the Mauro de Castro Secondary School through the intermediary of this research, could be replicated and extended to the daily life of other schools through the greater involvement of social actors and local authorities.

Finally, I would like to point out that the conclusions of this analysis are only partial, and represent a reflective contribution on utopias practiced towards paths that lead to a decolonial pedagogy in art/education, which, however, could be extended to other curricular areas and to education as a whole. Thinking about a decolonial option for knowledge and education requires considering the contributions of local histories and denied, marginalized and subalternized epistemologies. But perhaps more importantly, a political and ethical attention to our own practices and places of enunciation in relation to these histories and epistemologies, to the interventions we can undertake to build and generate political consciousness, decolonizing methodologies and critical pedagogies. If, as Walsh (2005) puts it, in order to confront the hegemony and coloniality of thought, it is necessary to confront and make visible our own subjectivities and practices, including our pedagogical practices, I believe that with this work I have achieved both epistemological and political gains in my own trajectory as a teacher and researcher.

REFERENCES

AGUIRRE, Imanol. **Imagining a future for Art Education**. 2009. Translated by Ines Rodrigues de Oliveira and Danilo de Assis Climaco. Available at:<http://pt.scribd.com/doc/60824348/Imaginando-um-futuro-para-a- educacao-artistica-Imanol-Aguirre>. Accessed on: August 20, 2011. Accessed on: May 13, 2013.

. Visual culture, the politics of aesthetics and emancipatory education. In: TOURINHO, I; MARTINS, R. (Orgs.). **Visual culture education**: concepts and contexts. Santa Maria, RS: UFSM, 2011. p.72-74.

AMARO, Ivan. Sexual Diversity, Difference and Curriculum: for a decolonial pedagogy in the peripheries. NATIONAL SEMINAR ON SEXUAL DIVERSITY EDUCATION AND HUMAN RIGHTS, 3, 2014. Vitoria, ES, 2014. **Proceedings**... Vitoria: [S.l], 2014. Available at: <http://www.gepsexualidades. com.br/resources/anais/4/1404606481_ARQUIVO_IVAN_AMARO_IIISEMINARIOE D UCACAO_DIVERSIDADESEXUAL_2014.pdf>. Accessed on: May 12, 2014.

ANDRADE, Oswald de. Manifesto antropofago. In: OBRAS Completas. Rio de Janeiro: Civilizagao brasileira, 1970. p. 13-19.

BARBOSA, Ana Mae; COUTINHO, Rejane G. Arte como cultura e a pos-modernidade. In: **Teaching art in Brazil**: historical and methodological aspects. Sao Paulo Teacher Training Network. Sao Paulo: UNESP, 2011. p. 4-6

BARRIENDOS, Joaquin. **La colonialidad del Ver**: Hacia un nuevo dialogo visual interepistemico. Nomadas, Bogota, n.35, 2011.Available at: <http://www. Scielo. org.co/scielo.php?script=sci_arttext&pid=S0121-75502011000200002&lng=en & nrm =iso>. Accessed on: 02 Apr. 2014.

BEZERRA. Heraldo. **O cerol fininho da Baixada**: Historias do cineclube Mate Com Angu. Rio de Janeiro: Aeroplano, 2013.

BHABHA, Homi. **The place of culture**. Belo Horizonte: Editora da UFMG, 2003.

BREDARIOLLI. Rita. Post-modern methodologies: art as expression and culture. In: **Methodologies** for teaching and learning art. Sao Paulo: Unesp, 2012.

CANDAU, Vera Maria. Educational Reforms in Latin America Today. In: MOREIRA, Antonio F. Barbosa (Org). **Curriculo**: politicas e praticas. Campinas: Papirus, 2001. p. 34.

_____. Multiculturalism and education: challenges for pedagogical practice. In: MOREIRA, A. F. and CANDAU, V.M.F. (eds.). **Multiculturalism:** cultural differences and pedagogical practices. Petropolis, RJ: Vozes, 2008. p. 55.

CANDAU, Vera Maria; RUSSO, Keli. Interculturality and Education in Latin America: a plural, original and complex construction. Curitiba: **Rev. Dialogo Educ.**, Campinas, v. 10, n. 29, Jan-Apr, 2010.

CASTRO-GOMEZ, Santiago; GROSFOGUEL, Ramon. Foreword. The decolonial turn: critical theory and heterarchical thinking. In: CASTRO-GOMEZ, Santiago; GROSFOGUEL, Ramon (Orgs.). **El Giro, decolonial**: reflexiones para una diversidad epistemica mas alla del capitalismo global. Bogota: Universidad Central/Pontificia and Universidad Javeriana, 2008. Page 9.

CERTEAU, Michel de, **Culture in the plural**. Trad. Enid Abreu Dobranszky - Colegao Travessia do seculo, Campinas: Papirus, 1995.

The invention of everyday life: 1. Arts of making. Petropolis: Vozes, 2008.

CHARREU, Leonardo. Visual Culture: breaking with curricular inertia and ignorance. In: TOURINHO, I. MARTINS, R. (Orgs.). **Visual culture education**: concepts and contexts. Santa Maria: UFSM, 2011. p. 122.

DUQUE DE CAXIAS. Municipal Department of Education. **Pedagogical proposal of the Duque de Caxias Department of Education**.V. 2. Duque de Caxias, 2004.

DUSSEL, Enrique. Europe, modernity and Eurocentrism. In: LANDER, Edgardo (Coord.) **La colonialidad del saber**: eurocentrismo y ciencias sociales, perspectivas latino-americanas. Buenos Aires: Clacso, 2000. p.29

GARCIA, Regina Leite. **Method, methods and counter-method**. Sao Paulo: Cortez, 2003.

GINZBURG, Carlo. **Myth, emblems, signs**: morphology and history. 2.ed.Sao Paulo: Companhia das Letras, 1989.

GIROUX, Henry. The disneyzation of children's culture. In: SILVA, Tomaz Tadeu da; MOREIRA, Antonio Flavio (Orgs.). **Contested territories:** the curriculum and the new political and cultural maps. Petropolis: Vozes, 2005. p. 25

GOMBRICH, E. H. **The History of Art**. 16 ed. Trad. Alvaro Cabral. Rio de Janeiro: LTC, 1999.

GOMEZ, Pedro Pablo. MIGNOLO, Walter (Orgs.). **Aesthetics and the decolonial option**. Bogota: Universidad Distrital Francisco Jose de Caldas, 2012.

HALL, Stuart. **Cultural identity in postmodernity**. Rio de Janeiro: DP &A. 2011.

HALL, Stuart. **From the diaspora**: identities and cultural media. Belo Horizonte: UFMG, 2013.

HARGREAVES, D. The knowledge-creating school. **British Journal of Educational Studies**, v. 47, n. 2, p. 122-144, 1999.

HERNANDEZ, FERNANDO. **Visual Culture, Educational Change and Work Projects.** Porto Alegre: Artmed, 2000.

JAGODZINSKI, Jan. Negotiations of difference: art education as disaffiliation in the postmodern era. IN: BARBOSA, Ana Mae e Guinsburg, J. (Orgs.). **Post-Modernism.** Sao Paulo: Perspectiva, 2008. p.667-685.

JOSGRILBERG, Fabio B. **Cotidiano e invengao**: os espagos de Michel de Certeau. Sao Paulo: Escrituras Editora, 2005.

LEON, Christian. Image, media and telecoloniality: towards a decolonial critique of visual studies. **Aisthesis** Santiago, n.51, 2012. Pontificia Universidad Catolica de Chile, Faculty of Philosophy. Available at: <http://www.scielo.cl/scielo. php?pid= S0718-71812012000100007&script=sci_arttext>. Accessed on: April 12, 2013.

LOPES, Alice Casimiro. Cultural pluralism in national curriculum policies. In: MOREIRA, Antonio F. B. (Org). **Curriculo**: politicas e praticas. Campinas: Papirus, 2001.

LOPES, Alice Casimiro; MACEDO, Elizabeth. **Theories of curriculum**. Sao Paulo: Cortez, 2011.

LOUREIRO. Celia Regina Nonato da Silva. **Emergencies and absences in the daily life of the learning laboratory at the Humaita I unit**. 2011. 127f. Master's dissertation in Education at the Faculty of Teacher Training, Rio de Janeiro State University, Sao Gongalo, 2011. Available at: <http://ppgedu.org/wp-content/uploads/2013/05/Disserta%C3%A7% C3% A3 o-C%C3%A9lia.pdf>. Accessed on: September 13, 2013.

MACEDO, Elizabeth Fernandes de Macedo. MOREIRA, Antonio Flavio Barbosa de. Does the concept of educational transfer still make sense? In: MOREIRA, Antonio F. B. (Org). **Curriculo**: politicas e praticas. 3. ed. Campinas: Papirus, 2001.

MALDONADO-TORRES. The topology of Being and the geopolitics of knowledge: Modernity, empire and coloniality. In: SANTOS, Boaventura de Sousa. MENESES, Maria Paula (eds.). **Epistemologies of the South**. Sao Paulo: Ed. Cortez, 2010.

MARIN, Jose. Interculturality and decolonization of knowledge: relations between local and universal knowledge in the context of globalization. **Visao Global**, Joagaba, v. 12, n. 2, 2009.

MARTINS, Raimundo. SERVIO Pablo Petit Passos. **Conflicts and ambiguities about cultural difference**: some impacts for postmodern art education and visual culture. Goiania: Federal University of Goias, 2013. Available at: <http://cascavel.ufsm.br/revistas/ojs-2.2.2/index.php/revislav/article/view/2553>. Accessed on: May 5, 2014. Page 5.

MCLAREN, Peter. **Critical Multiculturalism**. Sao Paulo: Cortez, 1997.

MENEZES. Andrea Penteado de. **The auditorium argument**: what do students say about art teaching in their schools? Thesis (Doctorate in Education, Faculty of Education), Federal University of Rio de Janeiro, Rio de Janeiro, 2009. Available at: <http://www.fe.ufrj.br/ppge/teses/andrea_penteado.pdf>. Accessed on: April 12, 2013.

MIGNOLO, Walter. **Local Histories/Global Projects**: coloniality, subaltern knowledges and liminal thinking. Translated by Solange Ribeiro de Oliveira. Belo Horizonte: UFMG, 2003.

. Coloniality from top to bottom: the western hemisphere on the conceptual horizon of modernity. In: LANDER, Edgardo (Org.) **The coloniality of knowledge**: Eurocentrism and the social sciences. Latin American perspectives. Consejo Latinoamericano de Ciencias Sociales. Buenos Aires: CLACSO, 2005. p.35

. **The idea of Latin America: the colonial legacy and the decolonial option**. Barcelona: Gedisa Editorial, 2007.

. Decolonial thinking: detachment and openness. A manifesto. In CASTRO-GOMEZ, Santiago and GROSFOGUEL, Ramon (Orgs.), **El Giro, decolonial.** Reflexiones para una diversidad epistemica mas alla del capitalismo global. Bogota: Universidad Central/Pontificia and Universidad Javeriana. 2008. p. 29

. Decolonial Aiesthesis. Articulo de reflexion. **Calle 14,** Bogota,v. 4, n. 4, p. 13 -25, jan. 2010.

. The New and the Decolonial. In: GOMEZ, Pedro Pablo; MIGNOLO, Walter (Orgs.). **Aesthetics and the decolonial option**. Bogota: Universidad Distrital Francisco Jose de Caldas, 2012. p.13.

NASCIMENTO, Erinaldo Alves do. Colonialities in the relationship between education and visualities.**Revista Digital do LAV**,Santa Maria,v. 6, n. 11,2013. Sep. 2013 Federal University of Santa Maria. Available at: <http://www.redalyc.org/pdf/3370/337028478006.pdf>. Accessed on: July 7, 2014.

OLIVEIRA, Ines B; AMORIM, Antonio Carlos Rodrigues de. (Orgs). **Meanings of curriculum**: between lines of theory, methodology and investigative experiences. Campinas: Anped, 2005. Available at: <https://www.fe.unicamp.br/gtcurriculo anped /documentos/LivroDigital_Amorim2006.p df>. Accessed on: June 2, 2013.

OLIVEIRA, Ines B. The arts of the curriculum. In: OLIVEIRA, Ines B. (Org.). **Alternativas emancipatorias em curriculo**. Sao Paulo: Cortez, 2004. p. 9.

. Boaventura de Souza Santos' contributions to curricular reflection: emancipatory principles and thought-practiced curricula. **E-curriculum**, Sao Paulo, v.8, n.2, 2012. Available at: <http://revistas.pucsp.br/index.php/curriculum/ articl e/view/10984.> Accessed on: September 18, 2013.

PAIS, Jose Machado. **Youth cultures**. Lisbon: Imprensa Nacional-Casa da Moeda, 2003.

QUIJANO, Anibal. Coloniality of power and social classification. **Journal of world-systems research**, v. 11, n. 2, 2000. Available at: <http://www.jwsr.org/ wp-content/uploads/2013/05/jwsr-v6n2-quijano.pdf.> Accessed on: May 3, 2014.

QUIJANO, Anibal. Coloniality of power, Eurocentrism and Latin America. In: LANDER, Edgardo (org). **The coloniality of knowledge**: Eurocentrism and social sciences. Latin American perspectives. Coleccion Sur Sur, Buenos Aires: CLACSO, 2005. p. 9.

RANCIERE, Jacques. **The sharing of the sensible**: aesthetics and politics. Sao Paulo: EXO experimental org. Ed. 34, 2005.

RICHTER, I. M. **Interculturalidade e estetica do cotidiano no ensino das artes visuais**. Campinas: Mercado das Letras, 2003.

. Multiculturalism and Interdisciplinarity. In: BARBOSA (Org.). **Inquietapoes e mudangas no ensino da arte**. 2.ed. Sao Paulo: Cortez, 2003b. p. 13-19.

RODRIGUES, Carla Cunha. **Meanings of difference in the discourses of contemporary Visual Arts teaching**. 2013. Dissertation (Master in: Education), Faculty of Education, Rio de Janeiro State University, Rio de Janeiro, 2013.

ROSAS, Ricardo. **Notes on artistic collectivism in Brazil**. 2005. Available at:<http://www.revistatropico.com.br/tropico/html/textos/2578,1.shl.> Accessed on: Feb. 24, 2015.

SANTOME, Jurjo Torres. The denied and silenced cultures of the curriculum. In: SILVA, Tomaz Tadeu da. **Aliens in the classroom**. Rio de Janeiro: Vozes, 1995. p. 159.

SANTOS. Boaventura de Souza. **Alice's hand**: the social and the political in post modernity. Sao Paulo: Cortez, 1995.

. **The critique of indolent reason**: against the waste of experience. Sao Paulo: Cortez, 2000.

_____. Introduction: broadening the canon of recognition, difference and equality. In: SANTOS, B. S. (Org.). **reconhecer para libertar:** os caminhos do cosmopolitanismo multicultural. Rio de Janeiro: Civilizagao Brasileira, 2003. p. 56.

. Towards a sociology of absences and a sociology of emergencies.In: SANTOS, B. S. **Prudent knowledge for a decent life**. Sao Paulo: Cortez, 2004. p. 2

. **From postmodern to postcolonial and beyond**. Coimbra: Center for Social Studies, Faculty of Economics, University of Coimbra, 2004. Available at: <http://www.ces.uc.pt/misc/Do_pos-moderno_ao_pos- colonial.pdf>. Accessed on October 15, 2014.

SANTOS. **Renovar la teoria critica y reinventar la emancipacion social.** Encuentros en Buenos Aires. Buenos Aires: CLACSO, 2006.

SHOHAT, Ella; STAM, Robert. **Critique of the Eurocentric Image**: Multiculturalism and Representation. Rio de Janeiro: Cosac & Naify, 2006. Page 451.

SILVA, Tomaz Tadeu da. **Documents of Identity**: an introduction to curriculum theories. 3 ed. Belo Horizonte: Autentica, 2011.

. The social production of identity and difference. In: **Identity and difference**: the perspective of cultural studies. Petropolis: Vozes, 2014.

SPIVAK, Gayatri Chakravorty. **Can the subaltern speak?** Petropolis: Vozes, 2005.

TLOSTANOVA, Madina. Transmodern aesthesis in the Eurasian borderland and the decolonial anti-sublime. In: GOMEZ, Pedro Pablo. MIGNOLO, Walter (Orgs.). **Aesthetics and the decolonial option**. Bogota: Universidad Distrital Francisco Jose de Caldas, 2012. p. 58-64.

VICTORIO FILHO, Aldo. Art teaching today: challenges, meanings and attunements. In: REUNIAO ANUAL DA ASSOCIAQAO NACIONAL DE POS-GRADUAQAO E PESQUISA EM EDUCAQAO, 31,2008.**GE1 Educapao e Arte...** Caxambu: ANPED, 2008. Available at: <http://31reuniao.anped.org.br/1trabalho/ GE01-4907-- Int.pdf>. Accessed on: June 12, 2013.

. The intimate utopia of education in the all-city: visual culture and training in the visual arts. In: TOURINHO, I; MARTINS, R. (Orgs.). **Visual culture education**: concepts and contexts. Santa Maria: UFSM, 2011. p. 204.

WALLERSTEIN. Emmanuel. **After Liberalism**. New York: New Press, 1995.

WALSH, Catherine. Interculturalidad, colonialidad y educacion. **Revista Educacion y Pedagogia,** Antioquia, Colombia, N. 48., 2007.Available at:<http://aprendeenlin ea.udea.edu.co/revistas/index.php/revistaeyp/article/view/6652>. Accessed on: July 7, 2014.

_____. Interculturality and the coloniality of power. An "other" thinking and positioning from colonial difference. In CASTRO-GOMEZ, Santiago and GROSFOGUEL, Ramon (Orgs.), **El Giro, decolonial:** reflexiones para una diversidad epistemica mas alla del capitalismo global. Bogota: Universidad Central/Pontificia and Universidad Javeriana, 2008. p. 28.

. Critical Interculturality/Decolonial Pedagogy. In: MEMORIAS del Seminario Internacional "Diversidad, Interculturalidad y Construccion de Ciudad", Bogota: Universidad Pedagogica Nacional, 2007. p.8.

Printed by Books on Demand GmbH, Norderstedt / Germany